HE JAVELIN

Martyn Chorlton

AMBERLEY

First published 2019

Amberley Publishing
The Hill, Stroud, Gloucestershire, GL5 4EP
www.amberley-books.com

Copyright © Martyn Chorlton, 2019

The right of Martyn Chorlton to be identified as the
Author of this work has been asserted in accordance with
the Copyright, Designs and Patents Act 1988.

ISBN 978 1 4456 8113 9 (print)
ISBN 978 1 4456 8114 6 (ebook)

British Library Cataloguing in Publication Data.
A catalogue record for this book is available from the
British Library.

Origination by Amberley Publishing.
Printed in Great Britain.

Contents

All-Weather Air Force   4

Straight Wing to Delta   5

A Gloster Design   7

Delta Wings   9

The Prototypes   11

Mark by Mark   19

Into Service   46

The Javelin 'In Action'   62

The Second Line Units   75

Technical Specifications   86

Units   89

Glossary   94

Bibliography   96

All-Weather Air Force

During the immediate period following the end of the Second World War, it quickly dawned on the Air Ministry that the capability of the bomber had rapidly developed since 1939 and bombers were capable of operating in virtually all conditions, day and night, at very high altitude. It also became clear that the early generation of jet fighter would have to be a 'maid of all work' and that the current inventory of fighter aircraft would not stand a chance of intercepting an enemy bomber without radar. With that in mind, the RAF could only provide adequate aerial defence of the UK using an aircraft with an all-weather capability and it would be the Gloster Aircraft Company who would deliver, albeit over a protracted period, their impressive delta-winged Javelin. The Javelin was destined to be Gloster's last production aircraft; the final one was delivered in 1960 although conversions continued until late 1961.

In service, the Javelin was a dependable and popular aircraft with its crews. It was more than adequate in the all-weather interceptor role until the arrival of the eye-watering English Electric Lightning, which literally took the RAF to a new level. It is probably because of the Lightning and its long career that the Javelin is somewhat overlooked and, when remembered, is given a host of nicknames (many of them unflattering) including the 'Flying Flat Iron'. With a service career that spanned from 1957 to 1975 and included service with twenty operational squadrons in the UK, Germany, the Near East and the Far East, all of which included a number of deployments, during which not a single shot (or missile) was fired in anger, the Javelin could be described as an underground success story.

Straight Wing to Delta

Aircraft design during the late 1940s was continually evolving and changing as knowledge in the field advanced rapidly. There was no defining moment when the Gloster engineers realised that their earlier straight-wing designs, such as the Meteor and E.1/44, would have performed better with a swept or, even more daringly, a delta wing. The development of aircraft during this period was very fluid and Gloster's new proposals for a single-seat and two-seat night and day fighter to the Ministry of Supply (MoS) were part of this resulting process. It was the designs that made the leap from the straight wing to the delta planform and the first of this new type of aircraft was presented in response to Specifications F.43/46 (OR.228) and F.44/46: the former for a single-seat day fighter, powered by Rolls-Royce AJ.65 or Metrovick F.9 axial engines, and the latter for a two-seat night/all-weather fighter. For F.43/46, Gloster developed three designs, the P.234, P.248 and P.250, while Hawker presented the P.1054. The first of two new operational requirements issued by the Air Ministry in December 1946, OR.227 (later F.4/48 in early 1948) looked for a two-seat night fighter to replace the Vampire in this role; the candidates for this would be

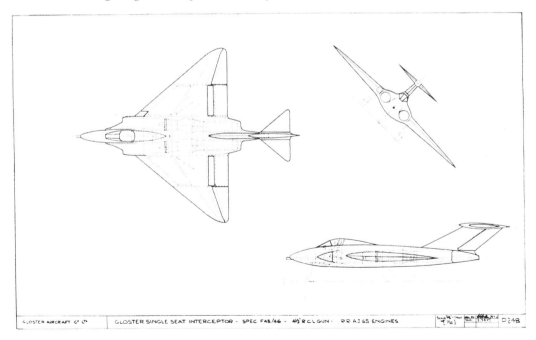

A drawing of the Gloster F.43/46 dated 13 August 1947, armed with a 4.5 in. recoilless gun and powered by a pair of Rolls-Royce AJ.65 engines. (Gloster Aircraft Co. Ltd)

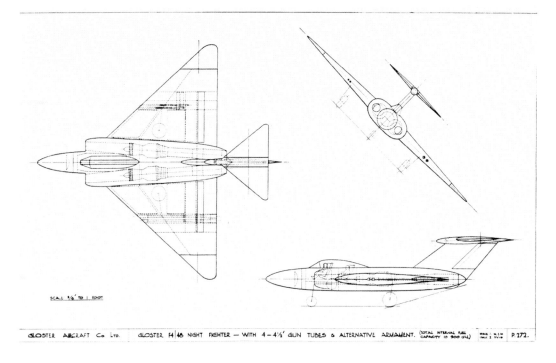

SCALE ⅛' TO 1 FOOT

GLOSTER AIRCRAFT Co LTD.   GLOSTER F4/48 NIGHT FIGHTER — WITH 4 – 4½' GUN TUBES & ALTERNATIVE ARMAMENT. (TOTAL INTERNAL FUEL CAPACITY 10 900 GAL)   P.272.

The Javelin takes shape, as seen in this drawing of the F.4/48 all-weather fighter dated 15 April 1948. (Gloster Aircraft Co. Ltd)

the de Havilland DH.110 (later Sea Vixen) and the Gloster Javelin. The second was OR.228 (later F.3/48 in early 1948) for a single-seat day fighter, which saw the evolution of the Hawker P.1067 into the superb Hawker Hunter, while the proposed Bristol Type 177 was destined not to leave the drawing board.

With regard to the earlier mentioned F.44/46, this specification evolved into F.24/48 (OR.258), again for a twin-engined, two-seat night/all-weather fighter which was very similar in appearance to the Meteor. Power was to be provided by a pair of 6,500 lb Rolls-Royce AJ.65 engines or a pair of 7,000 lb Metropolitan Vickers F.9 engines, which would later be known as the Avon and Sapphire respectively.

A Gloster Design

At first, the Javelin would be constructed in a similar fashion to the tried and tested methods adopted for the Meteor but would incorporate a swept wing with a 9 per cent thickness/chord ratio. Armament was initially planned as being a quartet of 30 mm guns or one 4.5 in. recoilless gun which was being developed at Fort Halstead in Kent. Other weapons which were considered at the time were the 57 mm Molins and the 40 mm Rolls-Royce and Vickers cannons. Eventually, the 30 mm Aden cannon was settled upon, pending the arrival of guided missiles, while the 4.5 in. recoilless gun was still left as an option on the table.

The earlier mentioned specifications, F.43/46 and F.44/46, created quite a stir throughout the British aircraft industry and by the time the Air Ministry drew a line under it, over fifty design proposals had been submitted, the vast majority of which were unrealistic if imaginative. The two operational requirements, OR.227 and 228, still stood but the Air Ministry put the brakes on while discussions were held with the aviation industry and a number of research establishments. It was clear that, despite information gleaned from Second World War scientists, not enough was known about subsonic fighter aircraft and, on top of that, very little government money was diverted to high-speed research. In the meantime, Gloster did not lose out as the Meteor NF.11, and later the NF.12 and NF.14, would fill the night-fighter void, along with the de Havilland Venom NF.3, while decisions and development continued.

Gloster's own contribution to Specification F.44/46 was a number of delta-winged designs. One in particular stood out: a two-seat design topped with a delta tailplane and armed with four 30 mm Aden cannon which was then designated with the Gloster project number P.238 (Day and night interceptor). The P.238 became the main focus of attention of the MoS and Directorate of Technical Development (DTD) and it was not long before they were sitting around the same table with Gloster's Chief Designer (soon to be Technical Director), George Carter. It was during one such meeting that the subject of armament arose and attention was turned towards to the 4.5 in. recoilless guns again rather than the 30 mm cannon, despite the former weighing 1,810 lbs each. An airborne radar with a 42 in. scanner was suggested as an installation in the nose, along with a variable incidence tailplane to give full control of the aircraft from flying speed to maximum speed. The proposed powerplant was a pair of 6,500 lb thrust Rolls-Royce AJ.65 engines which, on paper at least, were deemed powerful enough to propel the aircraft (weighing 25,000 lb) to Mach 0.9.

All of the above modifications were then applied to Gloster's follow-up design study, designated the P.272 (Two-seat night fighter with four 4.5 in. recoilless guns, dated 1948 ('Design Study')). The P.272 was put forward, which was an updated specification numbered F.4/48 (OR.227). During this process, opinions changed again with regard to the armament

The experimental delta-winged Boulton-Paul P.111, which arrived too late to influence the design of the Javelin. (R. L. Ward Collection)

and the 30 mm Aden cannons were offered as an alternative to the 4.5 in. recoilless gun. On top of that, better performance was in the offing as Gloster presented the P.272 with a pair of 9,000 lb Armstrong Siddeley Sapphire 2s instead of the AJ.65s.

Delta Wings

While the finer points regarding specifications were being pushed and pulled, RAE Farnborough set about investigating delta wings. While the Farnborough boffins worked hard on various designs, aided by access to wind tunnels, two aircraft manufacturers set about putting practice into theory. The first of them was Boulton Paul who, working closely with the RAE, were awarded a contract to Specification E.27/46 (OR.241) to build an experimental aircraft to investigate delta wing characteristics at transonic speeds. The aircraft was the tubby little P.111, which first flew on 10 October 1950. Installed with an incredibly thin 45 degree delta wing, this aircraft came too late to provide Gloster with any useful information before its own delta machine reached an advanced stage.

Avro also produced its own delta-winged development aircraft in the shape of the Avro 707 family, the first of which, the 707A, took to the air on 4 September 1949, again

The firstborn: the Avro 707A, one of several development aircraft which were created to explore the delta wing and would go on to benefit the Vulcan rather than the Javelin. (R. L. Ward Collection)

The Avro 707B, which first flew in September 1950, gave a number of test and research pilots their first taste of what it was like to fly a delta-wing aircraft. (R. L. Ward Collection)

too late to influence the Gloster machine, and to complicate matters further it was lost on 30 September. The 707B, which first flew on 6 September 1950, arrived in sufficient time to provide experience of flying a delta-winged aircraft (especially the low-speed characteristics) to Gloster test pilots, specifically Chief Test Pilot Sqn Ldr W. A. 'Bill' Waterton, who would be carrying out the maiden flight.

The Prototypes

Unlike many other aircraft manufacturers during this post-war period, Gloster was sitting pretty with healthy contracts already in place for the Meteor, which also included a further contract for night fighter variants that were sub-contracted out to Armstrong Whitworth. So the news that the DTD had accepted the P.272 in 'principle' in March 1948 was very encouraging for the company's short term future, if nothing else. Before an order for prototype aircraft could be placed, though, a number of changes to the design would be implemented. By July 1948, Gloster were settling on an aircraft which was powered by a pair of 9,000 lb Sapphire 2 engines but further proposals raised the aircraft's weight to 29,200 lb and the wing area from 900 to 1,100 sq. ft. Literally weeks later, the goal posts were moved again and the DTD proposal reverted to a 900 sq. ft wing with traditional power-boosted ailerons instead of wingtip controls. On top of that, the all-moving electrically actuated tailplane was to have powered elevators and the engines were changed to 7,500 lb Sapphire 3s. In the meantime, further good news was received as, in July, an order for four prototypes was placed at a cost of nearly £2 million.

George Carter made way for new Chief Designer Richard W. Walker in early 1949 and, on 13 April that year, Gloster received an 'Instruction to Proceed' from the Air Ministry. However, one of many poor decisions was made which would eventually cause the self-destruction of the British aviation industry when, in November 1949, the MoS decided to reduce the number of prototypes to just two! By then designated the GA.5, this short term economy measure caused untold upheaval to the aircraft's early development and, as a result, the MoS would reinstate the order to a total of five fighter prototypes and a single trainer. By the time this decision had been made, the first production aircraft was rolling off the production line, before the prototype order was completed!

Work began on the first prototype, serialled WD804, in April 1949. Further work began on the second prototype, serialled WD808, not long after with both being manufactured at the Hucclecote factory and assembled at Bentham. The main sub-assemblies were then transported to Gloster's test airfield at Moreton Valence for final assembly, which included installation of the engines and all of the systems. WD804 arrived at Moreton Valence in July 1951 and over the following three months, the aircraft was fully reassembled then ground tested and taxied for a further month before it was ready for its maiden flight. In the hands of 'Bill' Waterton, GA.5 WD804 took off on 26 November 1951 for a flight lasting no more than 34 minutes. It was far from being the perfect initial flight and Waterton reported severe rudder vibration and buffeting in flight which, following a ground inspection, exposed the fact that airflow was being disrupted around the rear fuselage and the jet pipes, which would have to be extended to eradicate this problem.

The GA.5 did not set the world aflame with its blistering performance and the F.4/48 specification called for a maximum speed of 605 mph at 40,000 ft and a service ceiling of 45,000 ft (to be reached in 10 minutes from start-up), none of which was achieved by WD804. In defence of the aircraft, these figures were never reachable thanks to down-rated engines and an unexpected weight increase of 700 lbs. In the meantime, flight testing continued with WD804, laden with test instrumentation plus an anti-spin parachute which was fitted within a streamlined fairing positioned on top of the large delta tailplane.

All was going well with testing until 29 June 1952 when, on WD804's ninety-ninth flight, Waterton experienced the loss of both elevators after a violent flutter. Determined not to abandon a valuable aircraft and all the autopilot records of the flight, Waterton carefully regained control of the aircraft and, after a couple of practice approaches, managed to land WD804, at speed, onto Boscombe Down's long main runway. The undercarriage collapsing was the only serious damage and Waterton managed, after a brief struggle, to open the canopy and walk away uninjured. For his skill, he was awarded the George Medal.

Regardless of this incident, and even before the second prototype GA.5 had flown, the MoS placed a production order for forty aircraft, to be named 'Javelin' and designated as F(AW).1s, the abbreviation equating to 'Fighter (All Weather), on 7 July 1952. Gloster found itself in the novel position of having no airworthy prototype aircraft but simultaneously preparing a production line for what was an aircraft that had not been fully proven. The lack of test aircraft was bridged on 21 August 1952 when the second prototype, WD808, made its maiden flight out of Moreton Valence, once again in the hands of Bill Waterton. Only days later, the GA.5 would make its public debut at the SBAC, Farnborough, and despite a number of flight restrictions being placed on the aircraft because of the loss of WD804, Waterton managed to demonstrate the aircraft low and slow, much to the appreciation of the crowd.

WT827 was the third prototype and first took to the air on 7 March 1953. This aircraft was the first to be armed, specifically with four 30 mm Aden cannon, and was also equipped with AI radar and a shaped radome to fit. WT827 would prove to be the most productive prototype to date, the aircraft taking part in a number of successful trials including gun heating and firing, general engineering, generator cooling, radome development and flight refuelling. For the latter, a large probe was installed on the starboard side of the aircraft, set so far back that inflight refuelling proved difficult.

Fuel, or lack of it, was always a problem with early interceptors and this factor was not lost on a couple of USAF test pilots who flew the GA.5 in March 1953 as part of the Mutual Defense Aid Program. The internal fuel capacity of the early fighter variants was 765 gallons, but to improve this, a pair of 250 gallon ventral tanks (aka 'bosom' tanks) were installed for the first time under WT827. These tanks would remain a feature of all marks up to 5, when the internal fuel capacity was improved and provision for pylon-mounted tanks was introduced.

As well as poor endurance, the handling of the GA.5 had been criticised by several pilots, especially at high altitude. The experience gained from flight testing and continuing wind-tunnel testing concluded that the aircraft would require a redesigned wing to improve its performance. As a result, the sweepback of the outer wing panels, outboard of the cannon bay, was reduced, giving a kinked appearance. This modification improved the tip stalling and increased the lift coefficient at high subsonic speeds. The new wing was installed on WD808, which was first flown on 28 May 1953, and was immediately found to be a significant improvement over the original design. Unfortunately, WD808 was destined to be lost on 11 June 1953 on its sixty-seventh flight with Lt Peter G. Lawrence RN MBE at the controls. In an accident that was not attributed to the new wing design, the aircraft was carrying out an elevator response trial at 15,500 ft and 125 kts with the flaps up. When the flaps were lowered, the aircraft entered a stable stall over Flax Bourton, south-west of Bristol, from which it did not recover. Lawrence unsuccessfully ejected at 400 ft and was killed after hitting the ground a mere 300 yds from his aircraft.

The fourth prototype was WT830, which was the first to benefit from powered ailerons and boosted elevators. Bill Waterton once again carried out the maiden flight, although this time it was from Hucclecote on 14 January 1954. WT830 went on to serve Gloster as an aerodynamic and stress research aircraft before joining the A&AEE at Boscombe Down until it was grounded in late 1959.

The last of the fighter prototypes was WT836, which made its maiden flight on 20 July 1954 in the hands of 'Dickie' Martin, who had recently taken over as Chief Test Pilot following Waterton's departure earlier that year. This aircraft looked more like an early production aircraft, the first of which would take to the air just two days later. The most obvious new feature was the 'high line' double transparent canopy, which gave sufficient clearance for the new style 'bone dome' helmets which were entering service. WT836 took part in a number of trials, many with the A&AEE, including hood jettisoning in the 'blower' rig at Boscombe Down.

The first prototype GA.5, WD804, at Hucclecote sporting the original delta-wing shape and jet pipe fairing. (Gloster Aircraft Co. Ltd via R. L. Ward Collection)

Above: A dramatic view of the first prototype, WD804, which was first flown by 'Bill' Waterton on 26 November 1951. (Gloster Aircraft Co. Ltd via R. L. Ward Collection)

Below: GA.5 WD804 had a short flying career; the aircraft was written off at Boscombe Down on 29 June 1952. 'Bill' Waterton stayed with the aircraft and saved the all-important automatic records on board. For this act he was awarded the George Medal. (Gloster Aircraft Co. Ltd via R. L. Ward Collection)

Above: The second prototype GA.5, WD808, was also destined to have a short flying career and this temporarily left Gloster Aircraft without a single operable prototype. (Gloster Aircraft Co. Ltd via R. L. Ward Collection)

Below: First flown on 21 August 1952, WD808 made its first public appearance at the SBAC, Farnborough, and is pictured on final approach into the Hampshire airfield. (Gloster Aircraft Co. Ltd via R. L. Ward Collection)

Above: The third prototype GA.5, WT827, was the first of the breed to be armed and was also fitted with an experimental 'bull-nose' radome. (Gloster Aircraft Co. Ltd via R. L. Ward Collection)

Below: Armed with four 30 mm Aden guns and equipped with AI radar, the third prototype was first flown on 7 March 1953. (Gloster Aircraft Co. Ltd via R. L. Ward Collection)

Right: Peter G. Lawrence, who left English Electric to work for Gloster, was the first pilot to lose his life in a Javelin accident. (R. L. Ward Collection)

Below: The first GA.5 to be fitted with full-power ailerons and boosted elevators, WT830 performed its maiden flight in the hands of 'Bill' Waterton on 14 January 1954. Note the revised wing shape. (Gloster Aircraft Co. Ltd via R. L. Ward Collection)

Above: Used by Gloster Aircraft for aerodynamic and stress research flying, WT830 ended her days as a ground trainer at RAF Bircham Newton before being SOC in November 1962. (Gloster Aircraft Co. Ltd via R. L. Ward Collection)

Below: The fifth and final fighter prototype was WT836, seen here under tow at Hucclecote. This aircraft made its maiden flight on 20 July 1954 with 'Dicky' Martin at the controls. (R. L. Ward Collection)

Mark by Mark

F(AW).1

The first production Javelin F(AW).1, XA544, was first flown by 'Dickie' Martin on 22 July 1954. Powered by a pair of 8,000 lb Sapphire Sa.6 engines, the F(AW).1 was also equipped with an AI Mk 17 radar (installed prior to RAF service at No. 23 MU, RAF Aldergrove) and featured an electrically operated variable incidence tailplane (from XA545). Of the forty F(AW).1s built, only twenty-nine were destined to be delivered to the RAF; because there was so much clearance and test flying still to be carried out, eleven were retained for a multitude of trials. These eleven would be retained as CA aircraft and, in summary, the aircraft were involved in the following trials: radar and gunnery (XA544); flying controls (XA545); Gee (XA546); Firestreak weapon pylons (XA547); anti-spin parachute/spinning trials (XA548); radar trials (XA549); 10,000 lb Gyron Junior engine trials with de Havilland (XA552); electrical (XA553); intensive flying (XA558); miscellaneous TIs (XA559); Sapphire Sa.7 reheat trials, ff. 30 September 1955 (XA560); anti-spin parachute and tail bumper bar with A&AEE (XA561); Avon RA.24 engines (XA562); handling (XA563); spinning trials (XA561); and radar trials (XA567).

XA544 and XA546 made their public debut at the SBAC, Farnborough, in September 1954. However, the latter was lost just over twelve months later. Flt Lt R. J. Ross of the RAE was allegedly attempting to recover from a spin which was deliberately initiated at low altitude. The Javelin's high descent rate of 240 ft/sec. must have caught the pilot out because the aircraft was witnessed crashing into the Bristol Channel off Weston-super-Mare, not far from an island called Steep Holm, on 21 October 1955. Neither the pilot nor the aircraft were ever recovered.

Overseas sales were in the offing very early on and a number of European air forces expressed an interest but all of the deals were lost thanks to more inviting packages being offered by US manufacturers. Development flying continued apace in 1955 and in June of that year XA556 flew the Gloster flag at the Paris Air Show. Demonstrated by Geoff Worrall (destined to be Gloster's last Chief Test Pilot), the aircraft very nearly did not perform thanks to damage to a jet pipe caused by a very wet start and then a flame-out while airborne. XA544 took part in the RAE Golden Jubilee at Farnborough while XA564 and XA565 appeared at the 1955 SBAC display, again at Farnborough. However, it was the RAF that Gloster was really trying to impress and the opportunity came with Operation Beware, the main annual air defence exercise, in which XA554 and XA559 took part. Both aircraft were fitted with a pair of 250-gallon 'bosom' tanks and operated out of RAF Coltishall in Norfolk. The aircraft impressed the crews that flew them and, more importantly, the attending Air Staff. Tasked with intercepting 'enemy' aircraft approaching the coast, the Javelins successfully claimed the destruction of several Canberras located approximately 100 miles from the coast and even managed to bounce a few unsuspecting USAF F-100 Super Sabres.

The all-important CA release of the Javelin F(AW).1 was received by Gloster on 30 November 1955. This meant that deliveries to the RAF could now begin and the first three to leave Moreton Valence departed for No. 23 MU at RAF Aldergrove on 30 December 1955.

Above: The first production Javelin F(AW).1, XA544, storms out of Moreton Valence. First flown on 22 July 1954, XA544 served with the RAE and the A&AEE before being relegated to ground trainer duties at RAF Cosford in December 1957. (Gloster Aircraft Co. Ltd via R. L. Ward Collection)

Below: Precision parking at Moreton Valence with F(AW).1 XA552 in the foreground, before it was converted by de Havilland into the Gyron Junior testbed. (R. L. Ward Collection)

Above: Captured at Moreton Valence and not all visible are Javelin F(AW).1s XA545 and XA548, F(AW).2 XA634 and the prototype T.3, WT831. (R. L. Ward Collection)

Below: One of eleven F(AW).1s that never entered operational service, XA546 was used for GEE trials. The aircraft went down in the Bristol Channel on 21 October 1954. The RAE pilot (attached to Gloster), Flt Lt R. J. Ross, was killed. (R. L. Ward Collection)

Above: The seventh production Javelin F(AW).1, XA550, which was retained by Gloster Aircraft for continued trial and development flying. (Gloster Aircraft Co. Ltd (P35-55 (Russell Adams) via Martin Richmond Photos)

Below: Javelin F(AW).1 XA564, which took part in the 1955 SBAC display at Farnborough. XA564 is a survivor, having been assigned as a ground trainer at RAF Cosford in April 1967. She was moved to the museum site in September 1975. (R. L. Ward Collection)

Above: F(AW).1s XA563 and XA564; the former served with the A&AEE at Boscombe Down on handling trials, and later with the RAE. She came to an undignified end at the RAF Catterick Fire School in 1965. (Gloster Aircraft Co. Ltd via R. L. Ward Collection)

Below: Another F(AW).1 held back from service was XA549, which carried out radar trials with the A&AEE. The aircraft did later serve with the CFE and No. 87 Squadron before serving as a ground trainer at RAF Swanton Morley. (R. L. Ward Collection)

Above: F(AW).1 XA552 on display at Farnborough. The aircraft was transferred to de Havilland for the fitment of a pair of 10,000 lb thrust Gyron Junior reheated engines. (R. L. Ward Collection)

Below: The final production Javelin F(AW).1, XA628, prior to delivery to No. 46 Squadron at RAF Odiham. (Gloster Aircraft Co. Ltd via R. L. Ward Collection)

Geoffrey Worrall, the Gloster
Aircraft Company's last Chief Test
Pilot. (R. L. Ward Collection)

F(AW).2

The first Javelin F(AW).2 was XD158 and this made its maiden flight on 31 October 1955, again in the hands of 'Dickie' Martin. The first of thirty production aircraft, XA768, first flew on 25 April 1956. The F(AW).2 differed from the F(AW).1 thanks to its radar, which was the American-built AI.22 (AN/APQ-43), and the introduction of an all-flying tail. Externally, the radome had a more asymmetric shape and, unlike the F(AW).1 nose, which had to be removed to gain access to the radar, the F(AW).2's was hinged.

The Javelin F(AW).2 received its CA release on 31 May 1957 and the first of twenty-six production aircraft were delivered to the RAF from 27 June, the type becoming operational with No. 46 Squadron from August 1957. The remaining four and the prototype, XD158, were held back for further test flying with Gloster and the A&AEE. These aircraft carried out the following trials: radar and generators (XA769); armament controls (XA770); missiles (XA771 and XA778 – pacer aircraft for A&AEE from March 1961); and radar trials (XD158).

Above: RAF Liaison Pilot for Javelin production and development, Sqn Ldr Peter Scott. (R. L. Ward Collection)

Below: Javelin F(AW).2 XA778 served solely with the A&AEE from August 1956 through to 1968. The fighter was operated as a pacer aircraft from March 1961 and was later used to test engines and F(AW).7 components. (R. L. Ward Collection)

Above: XA778 on final approach at RAF Boscombe Down. (R. L. Ward Collection)

Below: One of four production Javelin F(AW).2s that were held back for test duties was XA770, which had special armament controls installed. The aircraft is pictured here in 1961 at No. 23 MU, RAF Aldergrove, where it had been in open storage since December 1959. (Via E. Roffe)

T.3

For the benefit of this book and the natural order of things, the Mk 3 trainer variant is the next mark in this section. However, the prototype T.3 did not make its maiden flight until August 1956 and was preceded by the F(AW).4 and F(AW).5. This situation was yet another case of poor planning as you would have expected a dual-control trainer for the RAF's latest and largest fighter to enter operational service in time to be available from the outset for crew training and conversion.

Work began on the GA.5 trainer back in 1950 to OR.278, which called for an instrument, gunnery and pilot conversion aircraft. The initial design study considered a side-by-side cockpit but a more logical layout using the aircraft's existing tandem configuration and instrument arrangement was adopted. Making full use of the existing airframe, the trainer progressed under the Gloster Specification T.118D and was fundamentally based upon the forthcoming F(AW).6, complete with the same Sapphire Sa.6 engines and an all-flying tail. The T.3 had no radar and, to compensate for the rearward repositioning of the centre of gravity, the forward fuselage was extended by 44 in., a void that was conveniently filled with a pair of 50-gallon fuel tanks. The instructor's rear ejection seat was raised by 9.5 in. so that he had a good view forward and, as a result, the T.3 had a larger canopy than the operational fighters. The instructor also had a pair of horizontal periscopes on either side of the aircraft and, as the aircraft was designed for gunnery training, the T.3 was armed with four 30 mm Aden guns.

An order for twenty-two T.3s, under contract No.6/Aircraft/11262, was ordered on 27 September 1954, plus a single prototype serialled WT841. The construction of the latter was carried out by Gloster but was actually assembled by Air Service Training at Hamble. It was from the Hampshire airfield that the test pilot, Polish-born Jan Zurakowski, first flew the Javelin T.3 on 26 August 1956. The first production T.3, serialled XH390, made its maiden flight from Hucclecote on 6 January 1958, nearly two years after the F(AW).1 entered service.

The prototype trainer Javelin T.3, WT841, in close company with the first production F(AW).1, XA544. (Gloster Aircraft Co. Ltd (Russell Adams) via J. D. Transport Collectables)

Above: A gifted engineer, meticulous test pilot and superb display pilot, Jan Zurakowski was one of a kind and served Gloster Aircraft from 1947 to 1952. (R. L. Ward Collection)

Below: The prototype Javelin T.3 made its maiden flight in the capable hands of Jan Zurakowski on 26 August 1956. (Gloster Aircraft Co. Ltd (Russell Adams) via J. D. Transport Collectables)

Above: One of just twenty-two T.3 trainers built, this is XH395 'Z', in service with No. 46 Squadron at RAF Waterbeach on 19 September 1959. (R. L. Ward Collection)

Below: Javelin T.3 WT841 lining up for take-off at Farnborough in September 1956. The longer forward fuselage and more bulbous canopy gave the trainer very pleasing lines. (R. L. Ward Collection)

F(AW).4

As mentioned earlier, the next variant to actually enter operational service was the F(AW).4. Out of the fifty examples of this mark built, the first forty had a variable-incidence tailplane with standard power-boosted elevators. However, from the forty-first aircraft onwards, an all-moving tailplane was installed, as initially tested on the second production F(AW).1, XA545. In an effort to complete the flying and acceptance trials, F(AW).2 XA629 was moved from forty-first in the production line to number eleven and this aircraft was first flown by Peter Varley on 19 September 1955. The F(AW).4 was installed with the AI Mk 17 radar as per the F(AW).1 and was powered by a pair of Sapphire Sa.6 turbojets. The first eighteen of the production batch of fifty F(AW).4s were built by Gloster Aircraft and the remainder by Armstrong Whitworth at Baginton.

Twelve F(AW).4s were involved in trials work, including XA629, which was initially used for audible stall warning work but is better known for being fitted with a set of Kuchemann or Whitcombe 'bumps', which were more commonly referred to, by Gloster at least, as 'carrots'. The 'carrots' were large streamlined bodies which were mounted to the trailing edge of the wing and, later, were also installed on the wing tips. These 'bodies' were designed to reduce airflow separation and weaken shock waves at high, sub-Mach 1 speeds, therefore extending the buffet boundary. XA629 flew for the first time with the 'carrots' on 28 March 1956 and, in this guise, carried out 30 hours of flight testing. XA629 was also used for vortex-generator trials, of which two rows were placed along the leading edge of the outer wings and the trailing edge of each aileron was thickened. This modification produced the same positive results as the 'carrots' and, because the latter were considerably less obtrusive and much cheaper to produce and install, the generators were fitted to all further Javelins.

The second production Javelin F(AW).4, XA630, being readied for its maiden flight from Hucclecote on 29 March 1956. (Gloster Aircraft Co. Ltd via R. L. Ward Collection)

The F(AW).4 received its CA release on 7 December 1956 and, within a month, examples were being delivered to No. 141 Squadron. The remaining F(AW).4 trial aircraft were employed as follows: handling (XA630, XA632, XA634 and XA644); operational reliability (XA631); Climatic Det. (later CEFE), Nameo, Canada, for winterisation trials (XA720, XA721, XA723 and XA765); and served with the CFE (XA763 and XA764).

Above: Javelin F(AW).4 XA630, captured banking over Gloucester Cathedral. (Gloster Aircraft Co. Ltd via R. L. Ward Collection)

Left: Peter Varley, who became Assistant Chief Test Pilot for Gloster Aircraft from 1955. (R. L. Ward Collection)

Above: XA630 shows off a pair of 'bosom' ventral fuel tanks, each capable of holding an extra 250 gallons of fuel. (Via E. Roffe)

Below: No. 11 Squadron Javelin F(AW).4 XA756 'C', captured in west German skies in around late 1965. (R. L. Ward Collection)

Above: F(AW).4 XA634 was yet another trials aircraft held back for handling with both Glosters and the A&AEE. Having spent a number of years at RAF Leeming, XA634 has been saved and today resides at the Jet Age Museum. (R. L. Ward Collection)

Below: Javelin F(AW).4 XA632 pictured while serving Armstrong Whitworth prior to delivery to No. 11 Squadron at Geilenkirchen. (Gloster Aircraft Co. Ltd via R. L. Ward Collection)

F(AW).5

While externally it was nearly identical to the F(AW).4, the F(AW).5 was different on the inside thanks to the ability to carry more fuel, 125 gallons in each wing to be exact. Retaining the original AI Mk 17 radar, the F(AW).5 was also fitted with underwing pylons for the carriage of four de Havilland Firestreak air-to-air missiles.

XA641 was the first F(AW).5 to fly with 'Dickie' Martin in the cockpit on 26 July 1956. The CA release was issued on 4 March 1957, the type first being accepted by No. 151 Squadron at Leuchars on 2 April 1957. Once again, a number of aircraft were held back or diverted for trials work including the following: A&AEE trials (XA641, XA649 (Handling Sqn), XA709 and XA711 (gun firing)); CFE (XA642, XA648, XA665, XA668, XA696, XA697 and XA704; RAE (XA692 (IoAM)); and Armstrong Siddeley Motors Ltd (XA711).

The F(AW).5 was built in two production batches; the first was for fifty-eight aircraft built by Gloster Aircraft and the second, for just six aircraft, was carried out by Armstrong Whitworth at Baginton.

RAF visitors to an RNAS station in the shape a pair of No. 151 Squadron Javelin FAW.5s at Lossiemouth in 1959. (Via E. Roffe)

A very clean and smart Javelin F(AW).5, XA656, captured pre-delivery to No. 228 OCU in January 1957. (Gloster Aircraft Co. Ltd (Russell Adams) via J. D. Transport Collectables)

Above: Wg Cdr R. F. 'Dickie' Martin, who carried out a great deal of Javelin development flying and its introduction into RAF service. (R. L. Ward Collection)

Below: XH688 'X', a typical Javelin F(AW).5 in service with No. 151 Squadron, in around 1957. (Via E. Roffe)

Right: XA644 was a F(AW).5 which was credited as being delivered to the RAF in April 1956 but was not allocated a unit before it was lost in a mid-air collision with a Hunter on 24 August 1956. (Gloster Aircraft Co. Ltd (Russell Adams) via J. D. Transport Collectables)

Below: A once proud first production aircraft, F(AW).5 XA641 is pictured at No. 27 MU, RAF Shawbury, only weeks before it was scrapped. (Via E. Roffe)

F(AW).6

This variant was installed with the US AI.22 radar and, as a result, had a slightly modified radome in a similar style to the earlier F(AW).2. The first of thirty-three F(AW).6s, XA815, was first flown out of Hucclecote by 'Dickie' Martin on 14 December 1956. All Gloster-built, the F(AW).6 gained its CA release on 15 August 1957 and entered operational service with No. 89 Squadron the following month.

Just three F(AW).6s were used for trial work; these were with Gloster and the A&AEE, the latter for CA release (XA821), handling and fuel consumption checks with the A&AEE (XA834) and RAE (XA831).

Pristine No. 89 Squadron Javelin F(AW).6 XA815 'E', based at RAF Stradishall. (R. L. Ward Collection)

The larger radome of this Javelin gives it away as an AI.22-equipped F(AW).6. This example is XA775 'N' of No. 89 Squadron, in around 1958. (R. L. Ward Collection)

The last production Javelin F(AW).6, XA836, tucks up early and departs Hucclecote for delivery to No. 89 Squadron. (Gloster Aircraft Co. Ltd via R. L. Ward Collection)

F(AW).7

The arrival of the F(AW).7 was significant for the development and operational service of the Javelin as this variant was the first really fully capable example of the type to enter RAF service. The F(AW).7 encompassed all development work that had gone before and, as a result, more of this mark were produced than any other.

The F(AW).7 was the first Javelin to be able to operate with four air-to-air missiles and a pair of 30 mm Aden cannon as standard armament. Propelled to a maximum speed of 709 mph (Mach 0.92) by a pair of 11,000 lb Sapphire Sa.7 turbojets, the F(AW).7 weighed in at more than 40,000 lb with a full fuel load, which included a quartet of 100-gallon drop tanks under the wings and the two 250-gallon ventral tanks. The aircraft's flying control system was dramatically improved thanks to a Gloster-developed pitch auto-stabilisation system, a powered hydraulic rudder, a yaw stabiliser and an electro-hydraulic tri-axis autopilot which also included automatic altitude and approach control. The rear fuselage was extended slightly, the upper deck raised to reduce base drag, the vortex generators tested and thick trailing edge ailerons (tested on the F(AW).4) were installed. On top of that, the underwing pylons were carefully and extensively modified to reduce drag and, as a result, improve the aircraft's range. Despite these changes, this variant reverted to the AI Mk 17 radar.

F(AW).7 XH704 was the first of this new breed of Javelin to take to the air on 9 November 1956, again flown by 'Dickie' Martin. XH705 would serve as a 'try-out' aircraft for the Firestreak installation and it would not be until the thirtieth production aircraft, of a total of 142 built, that this system was fully integrated into the build. Later, all early production F(AW).7s were retrospectively fitted with the fully operational Firestreak system. Of the main production batch, twenty-four F(AW).7s would be used for a wide-ranging number of trials, including handling and auto-stabilisation; tropical; autopilot and vision in rain; missile and pitch stabilization to name a few, with a number of civilian and military establishments.

Production of the F(AW).7 was carried out by Gloster Aircraft and Armstrong Whitworth with overlapping serials. Deliveries to the RAF, via the MUs, began on 30 May 1958 and operationally to No. 33 Squadron from July 1958.

Javelin F(AW).7 XH714 lifts out of Hucclecote, possibly bound for its one and only posting to the A&AEE at Boscombe Down in November 1957. (Gloster Aircraft Co. Ltd via R. L. Ward Collection)

The first variant to be armed with a quartet of de Havilland Firestreak missiles, this F(AW).7, XH782, is in service with the GWDS (Guided Weapons Development Squadron), trialling its new capability. (R. L. Ward Collection)

A close-up of the tools available to the F(AW).7, including the Firestreak missile and rocket pod. (R. L. Ward Collection)

F(AW).7 XH712 displaying a metal nose fairing, complete with a pitot and yaw vane boom, a configuration for handling trials with the A&AEE. The aircraft was also involved in Firestreak and Red Top missile trials. (R. L. Ward Collection)

A lovely study of Javelin F(AW).7 XH756. (Via Chris Hearn)

F(AW).8

The last production Javelin to be built and the most powerful, thanks to its partially reheated 11,000 lb Sapphire Sa.7R engines, the F(AW).8 would mark the end of an era for Gloster Aircraft. The reheat system, which was operable above 20,000 ft, gave the F(AW).8 an additional 12 per cent of thrust, which equated to a total of 12,300 lb. The aircraft further advanced the Javelin design by being fitted with a Gloster-developed pitch auto-stabiliser, a Louis Newmark yaw stabiliser, a powered rudder, a drooping leading edge to the main wing, complete with two rows of Vortex generators, and, last but not least, a Sperry autopilot. The F(AW).8 was fitted with AI.22 radar and, armament-wise, could carry four Firestreaks and a pair of 30 mm Aden guns, although the latter were re-positioned to the outer mainplane.

Forty-seven F(AW).8s were built, all by Gloster Aircraft; the first of them, XH966, was flown for the first time by 'Dickie' Martin on 9 May 1958. Significantly, the last of this batch, XJ165, departed Moreton Valence on 16 August 1960 and was the last aircraft to be built by Gloster. The first examples were received by the RAF, via MUs, from 1 October 1959 and were in service by early 1960.

Out of the forty-seven built, four F(AW).8s were retained by Gloster Aircraft for CA release work and, later, auto-stabiliser trials and a further five were operated by the A&AEE for handling, performance and many other trials. A single aircraft, XJ125, was allocated to Armstrong Siddeley for development work with the Sapphire Sa.7R turbojet.

The first production F(AW).8, XH966, which first flew on 9 May 1958 with 'Dickie' Martin at the controls. (Gloster Aircraft Co. Ltd via R. L. Ward Collection)

A regular sight at the then annual SBAC display at Farnborough during the late 1950s and early 1960s, Javelin F(AW).8 XJ125 lines up for another display in 1961. (Via E. Roffe)

Javelin F(AW).8 XH966 was retained by Glosters for CA release work and went on to serve the A&AEE and No. 41 Squadron until it was withdrawn from use in February 1964. (Via E. Roffe)

Keeping a close eye on the competition. Javelin F(AW).8 XH979 holds a tight formation with its AFDS (Air Fighting Development Squadron) colleagues, including the type's ultimate replacement, the Lighting in the foreground. (R. L. Ward Collection)

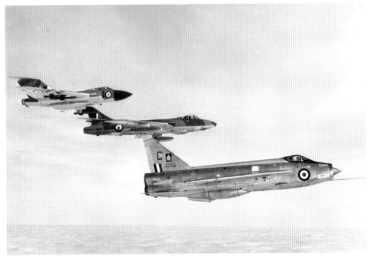

F(AW).9

The F(AW).7 was performing well in squadron service and its only failing was a lack of manoeuvrability at high altitude compared to its immediate successor, the F(AW).8. With that in mind, it was decided to 'upgrade' all F(AW).7s to the standard of the F(AW).8, which had yet to leave the production line, a number that totalled seventy-six aircraft. This batch were re-designated the F(AW).9 and the first to be converted was XH959 on 15 January 1960. A further twenty-two F(AW).9s were also modified with a 20-foot-long refuelling probe mounted on the starboard side of the fuselage, enabling these Javelins to fly as far afield as Singapore via air-to-air refuelling; these aircraft were re-designated the F(AW).9R.

Originally built as an F(AW).7, XH881 left the factory as an F(AW).9 and was delivered to No. 25 Squadron, based at RAF Waterbeach, in April 1960. (Crown Copyright via R. L. Ward Collection)

Above: No. 64 Squadron Javelin F(AW).9 XH844 on final approach into RAF Duxford in around 1962. (Via E. Roffe)

Below: The No. 64 Squadron line at RAF Duxford shows three F(AW).9Rs, including XH762 'F' in the foreground. XH762 later joined No. 29 Squadron and, after being in storage at RAF Shawbury, was sold for scrap in April 1968. (Via E. Roffe)

Into Service

The first trio of Javelins to leave Moreton Valence on 30 December 1955, were F(AW).1s XA568, XA570 and XA572, which were delivered to No. 23 MU at RAF Aldergrove, located on the north-eastern side of Loch Neagh in Northern Ireland. It was at No. 23 MU that the AI Mk 17 radar was installed and, following a number of routine checks, the first aircraft was delivered to No. 46 Squadron at Odiham on 29 February 1956.

First formed as a fighter unit on 19 April 1916, No. 46 Squadron saw a great deal of action during the First World War, claiming 184 aerial victories and creating seventeen aces before it was disbanded on 31 December 1919. Reformed at Kenley in September 1936 as part of the RAF Expansion Scheme, again as a fighter unit, No. 46 Squadron served in this role (and as a night fighter squadron from May 1942) until December 1944, when it was disbanded and reformed again as a transport unit flying the Short Stirling and later the Douglas Dakota which supported the Berlin Airlift. Disbanded in February 1950, No. 46 Squadron reformed again with the Armstrong Whitworth Meteor NF.12 and NF.14 at RAF Odiham on 15 August 1954, once again in the night fighter role and under the command of Sqn Ldr D. F. C. Ross.

It was under Sqn Ldr Ross that the first Javelin F(AW).1s arrived. To aid the conversion of crews, in lieu of a Javelin trainer eight Meteor NF.11s were also delivered while the unit's NF.12s were passed on to No. 72 Squadron. Sqn Ldr Ross was later replaced by Wg Cdr F. E. W. Birchfield, OBE, DFC, AFC. Birchfield was a highly experienced pilot who joined the RAF in 1937 and had, during his long career, commanded Nos 92 and 234 Squadrons. Following a night fighter conversion course with No. 228 OCU in January 1955, Birchfield was posted to Odiham on 23 March 1955 and, twelve months later, would take command of the RAF's first delta all-weather fighter squadron.

By May 1956, all of No. 46 Squadron's crews had been converted to the Javelin F(AW).1, meaning that the unit was perfectly prepared to serve as a proving squadron for this new aircraft. By this time, fifteen Javelins were on strength and eight of them had been designated for use as trials aircraft. The squadron's task was to reach 1,000 flying hours as quickly as possible and, to achieve this, two pairs of Javelins took off every day at from 0830 hrs through to 1430 hrs, every 30 minutes. Every conceivable operational procedure was carried out and the magic number of 1,000 flying hours was reached in under eight weeks. This was an incredible achievement. However, the task came at a cost when Wg Cdr Birchfield and his navigator, Fg Off. B. Chambers, were returning to Odiham in F(AW).1 XA570 'B' from a night interception exercise on 11 June 1956. A mere 1.5 miles ESE of the airfield, the Javelin inexplicably crashed into a small wood, killing both crew instantly.

Wg Cdr H. E. White DFC, AFC took over as Commanding Officer and No. 46 Squadron settled into a routine period of operational flying which was often disrupted by poor serviceability and a lack of spares. However, No. 46 Squadron would continue to be selected for a number of flying trials and take part in all of RAF Fighter Command's major exercises, which were prolific during the 1950s and beyond as the Cold War continued to drop in temperature. No. 46 Squadron operated the F(AW).1 until the summer of 1957, when the mark was transferred to No. 87 Squadron, operating out of RAF Brüggen in West Germany, in place of the Meteor NF.11. The first of fourteen aircraft, XA623, was delivered to Brüggen on 2 August 1957 and the unit would continue to operate the F(AW).1 until 1961, when it was replaced by the Javelin F(AW).5. Nos 46 and 87 Squadrons were destined to be the only operational squadrons to operate the F(AW).1.

As touched upon earlier, the next Javelin variant to enter RAF service was not the expected F(AW).2 but the F(AW).4, which first joined No. 141 Squadron at Horsham St Faith (pending runway resurfacing at their home station of RAF Coltishall) on 3 January 1957, in place of the Venom NF.3. No. 141 Squadron's transition to the Javelin was very smooth because several experienced flight commanders had been posted in from No. 46 Squadron. On their return to Coltishall, No. 141 Squadron quickly became operational on the F(AW).4 and within a short period the unit could take part in the RAF's immediate readiness role as part of Operation Fabulous. This operation was solely handled by Fighter Command and involved aircraft parked at 'readiness', with the crews strapped into the cockpit (for an hour at a time) ready to scramble and intercept the approaching Soviet threat. There was a 'Day Fab' and 'Night Fab', the latter now being handled by the Javelin. It was poetic that No. 141 Squadron, the RAF's longest-serving night fighter unit, should be the first to take up this role with the Javelin.

The F(AW).4 served with more operational squadrons than any other mark, including Nos 3, 11, 23, 41, 72, 87, 96 and 141 Squadrons, the latter being renumbered as No. 41 Squadron on 3 January 1957 but remaining at Coltishall. The F(AW).4 had a short operational career and was withdrawn from squadron service in March 1962 by No. 11 Squadron at Geilenkirchen, the unit having already fully converted to the F(AW).5 back in August 1961.

The honour of receiving the first F(AW).5 into RAF service went to another old night fighter unit, No. 151 Squadron at Turnhouse, who traded in their Venom NF.3s on 2 April 1957. No. 151 Squadron remained as part of Scotland's defence force until it was disbanded on 19 September 1961. Like the F(AW).4 before it, the F(AW).5, despite its improved capability, had a short service career, mainly because of the rapid development of the aircraft once in service. As a result, the mark only served until December 1962, when it was withdrawn by No. 11 Squadron at Geilenkirchen.

The first F(AW).2s did not enter operational service until August 1957, when they joined No. 46 Squadron to replace their F(AW).1s. Firmly entrenched at Odiham, No. 46 Squadron's serviceability record did not improve with the new mark, although a brief period with the F(AW).6 from May to October 1958 was appreciated. Only one of three operational squadrons to operate the F(AW).2, the others being Nos 85 and 89 Squadrons, No. 46 Squadron retained the F(AW).2 until it was disbanded on 30 June 1961, its nucleus remaining behind to ferry aircraft to the Far East for No. 60 Squadron.

No. 89 Squadron at Stradishall, which was reformed with the Venom NF.3 on 15 December 1955, was the first operational unit to receive the Javelin F(AW).6 in October 1957. On paper, at least, the situation was to prove short-lived as No. 89 Squadron was renumbered as No. 85 Squadron in November 1958, the latter unit continuing to operate the F(AW).6 out of RAF West Malling until June 1960. The only other operational unit to fly the F(AW).6 was No. 29 Squadron, from November 1957 until August 1961, out of RAF Leuchars.

Considering the amount of operational activity that has gone before us, it now seems strange to talk about the Javelin T.3. The long-awaited trainer variant of the Javelin entered service with No. 228 OCU at Leeming in October 1957, the unit having been first formed back in May 1947 as No. 228 (Tactical Light Bomber & Night Fighter) OCU. Even at this early stage of the Javelin's career, plans were afoot to phase the type out of RAF service as No. 228 OCU was disbanded, prematurely, on 15 September 1961. It was thought at this point in time that sufficient crews had been trained on the Javelin to see the aircraft out of service but an unexpected situation in the Far East resulted in a rethink. Nos 60 and 64 Squadrons were working hard protecting Malaysian airspace during the conflict with Indonesia and, as a result, there was clearly still a demand for two-seat fighters in the region. Therefore No. 228 OCU was reformed on 1 June 1965, this time at Leuchars, with a quartet of T.3s, nine F(AW).9s and three Canberra T.11s in support. The T.3s remained on strength until it was once again disbanded on 23 December 1966, becoming the last RAF unit to fly the Javelin on a regular basis in the United Kingdom.

Despite only twenty-three examples of the Javelin T.3 being built, it was a type that certainly did the rounds and examples served for varying lengths of time with Nos 5, 11, 23, 25, 29, 33, 41, 46, 60, 64, 72, 85, 96 and 151 Squadrons.

The Firestreak-armed F(AW).7 was the next to enter service. The first examples were delivered to the RAF on 30 May 1958. No. 33 Squadron, based at RAF Middleton St George and tasked with the all-weather aerial defence of the north of England, was the first operational unit to receive the F(AW).7 in July 1958. No. 33 Squadron continued this task until it was disbanded on 18 November 1962. Some of the aircrews were transferred to No. 5 Squadron, then based at Laarbrüch. No. 23 Squadron, a Javelin unit since March 1957, was unique because it operated the F(AW).7 twice, first from April 1959 to July 1960 and then again from April to September 1962, bridging the gap between the F(AW).4 and the F(AW).9R. No. 23 Squadron, operating from Horsham St Faith and Coltishall, was also the last unit to operate the F(AW).7. The only other unit to operate the mark was No. 25 Squadron, firstly at Waterbeach and later at Leuchars.

Next up was the final production version, the F(AW).8, which was delivered to RAF MUs from 1 October 1959 and was operational with No. 41 Squadron at Wattisham by the following month and with No. 85 Squadron at West Malling from March 1960. These two units were destined to become the only ones to operate the F(AW).8, No. 41 Squadron until 6 December 1963, when it was disbanded.

The last member of the Javelin family was the F(AW).9 and the first examples joined No. 25 Squadron at Waterbeach in December 1959, a mere four years after the F(AW).1 entered service, such was the rapid development of the Javelin. The F(AW).9 was by far the longest serving of the fighter variants although this still only covered a period of less than nine years before it was completely superseded by the English Electric Lightning. The in-flight refuelling variant, the F(AW).9R, was first put through its paces when a quartet of No. 23 Squadron aircraft flew non-stop to Singapore supported by Vickers Valiant tankers. No. 23 Squadron was destined to become the last United Kingdom-based unit to operate the Javelin when, in October 1964, the type was replaced by the Lightning.

No. 11 Squadron operated the Javelin F(AW).9 over West Germany between December 1962 and January 1966 while No. 29 Squadron at RAF Akrotiri withdrew the type in May 1967; the former disbanded and the latter converted to the Lightning. This just left the busy aircraft of Nos 60 and 64 Squadron in the Far East, which would soldier on until April 1968 and June 1967 respectively, both being disbanded at RAF Tengah, Singapore.

Above: A cracking formation of No. 46 Squadron Javelin F(AW).1s made up of XA626 'Q', XA627 'B', XA623 'G' and XA632 'D'. (Gloster Aircraft Co. Ltd (Russell Adams) via J. D. Transport Collectables)

Below: No. 46 Squadron Javelin F(AW).1s XA621 and XA622 'S' at RAF Odiham on 7 June 1957. (*The Aeroplane* via Martin Richmond Photos)

The flag-wavers for the RAF's newest, biggest fighter, not to mention the world's first twin-jet delta-wing fighter, No. 46 Squadron had plenty to show off about. (Gloster Aircraft Co. Ltd via R. L. Ward Collection)

Farewell to the Meteor NF.12 and welcome to the Javelin F(AW).1, as presented here with this No. 87 Squadron formation in September 1957. (Crown Copyright (596-8) via Martin Richmond Photos)

No. 87 Squadron
Javelin F(AW).1
XA565 'A' at
RAF Gaydon on
17 September
1960. (R. L. Ward
Collection)

No. 141 Squadron
Javelin F(AW).4
XA759 shows
off its clean lines
to the camera.
No. 141 Squadron
operated the
Javelin from
February 1957
until January
1958, when it was
renumbered as
No. 41 Squadron.
(R. L. Ward
Collection)

No. 141 Squadron
Javelin F(AW).4
XA639 at RAF
Coltishall. (R. L.
Ward Collection)

Above: No. 23 Squadron Javelin F(AW).4 XA731 on display at RAF Burtonwood on 18 May 1957. (R. L. Ward Collection)

Below: No. 72 Squadron Javelin F(AW).4 XA755 'H' taxiing at RAF Leconfield. (R. L. Ward Collection)

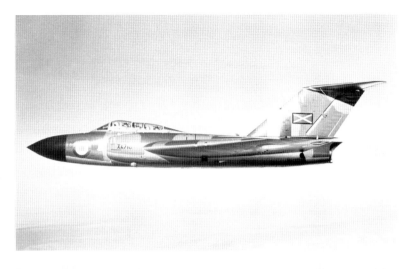

No. 151 Squadron Javelin F(AW).6 XA710 'Y' at altitude. (MoD (PRB.18505), R. L. Ward Collection)

No. 41 Squadron Javelin F(AW).5 XA658 'X' on the line at RAF Wattisham in around 1959. (R. L. Ward Collection)

A line of nine No. 46 Squadron Javelin F(AW).2s at RAF Odiham in the summer of 1957. (R. L. Ward Collection)

Above: A rare image of a No. 46 Squadron F(AW).2 on the move at RAF Odiham. This is XA807 'P', which sadly ended its days as a target at Foulness. (R. L. Ward Collection)

Below: A pair of No. 85 Squadron Javelin F(AW).6s, including XA832 'S', dispersed at RAF Stradishall. (Via E. Roffe)

Above: The prototype Javelin T.3, WT841, being put through its paces at the SBAC display at Farnborough. (*The Aeroplane* via Martin Richmond Photos)

Below: Another view of the T.3 trainer's pleasing lines thanks to the modification of the forward fuselage. (R. L. Ward Collection)

Above: Javelin T.3 XH437 served briefly with No. 33 Squadron before being passed on to No. 23 Squadron. The aircraft, like many Javelins, was written off following a starter fire. (R. L. Ward Collection)

Below: F(AW).7 XH837 'T' of No. 33 Squadron at RAF Lindholme in 1958. (R. L. Ward Collection)

Flt Lt Donald Christmas carries out his pre-flight checks on No. 23 Squadron Javelin FAW.7 'C' (XH758 or XH849) in May 1963. (Air Ministry (PRB.25288))

A lovely formation of No. 64 Squadron Javelin F(AW).7s. (Crown Copyright (PRB.36610) via Martin Richmond Photos)

No. 5 Squadron Javelin F(AW).5 XA707 'B' at dispersal at RAF Laarbrüch, West Germany. (Via E. Roffe)

Above: No. 23 Squadron F(AW).9 XH894 'R' between sorties in the foreground and No. 74 Squadron's Lightnings on the line at RAF Coltishall. (Via Mick Jennings)

Below: No. 85 Squadron Javelin F(AW).8 XJ116 'X' at RAF West Malling in 1960. (Via E. Roffe)

A tight four-ship display of No. 41 Squadron Javelin F(AW).8s. No. 41 Squadron operated three marks of the delta-winged fighter over a five-year period. (Crown Copyright (PRB.26106) via Martin Richmond Photos)

A typical Cold War Fighter Command station. This is an aerial view of RAF Wattisham taken on 10 June 1963. In residence are the Javelin F(AW).8s of No. 41 Squadron and the Lightnings of No. 111 Squadron. (Crown Copyright via Chris Hearn)

Above: No. 25 Squadron armourers remove the Firestreak air-to-air missiles from the Commanding Officer's personal Javelin F(AW).9, XH880 'JHW' (Wg Cdr J. H. Walton AFC), at RAF Waterbeach in around 1961. (Via Martin Richmond Photos)

Below: No. 25 Squadron introduced the Javelin F(AW).9 into service at RAF Waterbeach in December 1959. This aircraft is XH760 'B', which later served with No. 11 Squadron. (Via E. Roffe)

Above: The Commanding Officer, Wg Cdr J. H. Walton ('JHW'), of No. 25 Squadron leads a trio of Javelin F(AW).9s over Essex. Note Woodbridge and Bentwaters, across the border in Suffolk, in the background. (R. L. Ward Collection)

Below: No. 64 Squadron Javelin F(AW).9R XH849 'H' shows off its huge refuelling probe. (R. L. Ward Collection)

The Javelin 'In Action'

Being a product of the Cold War, the Javelin was very fortunate never to have been involved in a conflict during its operational service career. The majority of home-based squadrons serving with Fighter Command during their Javelin period would have been involved in a seemingly endless round of QRAs (Quick Reaction Alerts) and PIs (Practice Interceptions), not to mention a large number of exercises. The latter would have included Fighter Command and NATO-organised exercises plus a number of squadron exchanges.

In West Germany, the potential for scrambles and a resulting interception was much higher, although the four Javelin units, Nos 3, 11, 87 and 96 Squadrons, which covered a period from February 1958 until January 1966, had to compete with a number of other NATO air forces, including the USAF, who all had their own 'Battle Flight' arrangement.

The following is a summary of the Javelin's more interesting deployments and encounters.

Berlin 1961–62

In the summer of 1961, the Soviets threatened to blockade Berlin again and, to bolster the four squadrons already in place, two more were sent from the UK. These were No. 41 Squadron, who sent a dozen aircraft to RAF Geilenkirchen in August, and No. 85 Squadron, who moved to RAF Laarbrüch in September 1961. No. 29 Squadron also took a turn to deploy to West Germany, the unit arriving before Christmas at Geilenkirchen. The crisis continued into 1962 and the need to call upon RAF fighters to keep the Berlin air corridors clear still remained a possibility. No. 33 Squadron also took a turn with a four-month detachment with four Javelins at RAF Gütersloh, an airfield that was considerably closer to the Berlin corridors. The Luftwaffe also made Celle available for the No. 33 Squadron commitment, which took a hit when one of their four aircraft, F(AW).9 XH794, overshot the runway at Wildenrath on 9 March 1962 following a hydraulics failure.

A dozen Javelin F(AW).8s of No. 41 Squadron joined the West German party when they arrived at Gütersloh on 3 April 1962. This was bolstered by a further three aircraft the following day, which actually gave No. 41 Squadron the capability to put together a flying programme as well as maintaining a high state of readiness. By late 1962, the tension had subsided and the UK-based units began to return to normal again while those at the 'sharp end' in West Germany waited for the next crisis to take place.

The Far East 1961–68

Originally equipped with the Meteor NF.14, No. 60 Squadron, based at RAF Tengah, Singapore, began to receive the much-awaited Javelin F(AW).9 from July 1961. Actually delivering the aircraft to the Far East was a major logistical challenge which involved a two-stage deployment, flying from RAF Waterbeach through Istres, Luqa, El Adem, Diyabakir, Tehran, Bahrain, Sharjah, Masirah, Karachi, New Delhi, Benares, Calcutta, Rangoon, Bangkok, Butterworth and finally Tengah. This epic journey was not achieved without loss – of the second batch of aircraft to head east, one was damaged in a refuelling accident and F(AW).9 XH791 went down over the Ganges Delta on 5 August 1961 with the loss of the pilot.

By September 1961, No. 60 Squadron had a dozen Javelins on strength, which was a sufficient number to take part in a number of exercises and detachments before the unit's first real operational task. This came on 23 May 1962, when the squadron was ordered to come to 15 minutes' readiness because the Indonesian Air Force was equipped with the AS-1 air-to-surface missile-armed Tupolev Tu-16KS 'Badger'. Based at Medan in Northern Sumatra, these were the first examples of the Tu-16 to be seen operating outside of the Soviet Union and they posed quite a threat. A pair of Javelins had been deployed to Butterworth and they scrambled for the first time on 29 May but the Tu-16s remained inside Indonesian airspace, well clear of the approaching No. 60 Squadron aircraft. More Tu-16s were delivered to the Indonesian Air Force in June and this time a pair of No. 60 Squadron Javelins managed to intercept five of them between them, taking photographs to confirm.

Tension in the region continued to mount when, in January 1963, a policy of 'Confrontation' was announced by the Indonesian government. In response, Operation Tramp was initiated and No. 60 Squadron was ordered to provide 24-hour QRA, which was made up of a pair of fully armed Javelins at permanent 30 minutes' readiness. By September 1963, Operation Tramp was increased to six Javelins and, from 21 October, Tramp was increased further with two aircraft at 2 minutes' readiness at Butterworth. The latter scenario was alleviated slightly thanks to the Sabres of No. 77 Squadron, RAAF, based at Butterworth, who covered the daylight hours while the No. 60 Squadron detachment covered the nights. By November 1963, a four-strong detachment from No. 64 Squadron, who were already in India, was diverted to support Operation Tramp; this was a sign of things to come because No. 64 Squadron was based at Binbrook at this time but would later be moved in its entirety to Tengah. No. 60 Squadron's area of operations continued to grow as, by late 1963, they also included Borneo. The answer was to create a new 'C' Flight at Butterworth, which was duly equipped with four F(AW).9Rs, led by Sqn Ldr J. G. Ince, and operated by No. 23 Squadron crews under the banner of Operation Merino. The longer range F(AW).9R was greatly appreciated in the region and raised the number of operational Javelins at Butterworth to eight.

During the early hours of 25 February 1964, the Sarawak and Sabah boundaries were declared as an ADIZ thanks to an Indonesian declaration that they would supply guerrilla forces in Borneo from the air. As a result, the OC of No. 60 Squadron led a pair of Javelins and a detachment of No. 20 Squadron Hawker Hunters 400 miles east of Tengah to Kuching and a further four Javelins were relocated to RAF Labuan, another 360 miles further away. The Javelins were kept at a high state of readiness and a number of low-level standing patrols were flown, not to mention escort duties for RAF and RNZAF transport aircraft on supply drops.

Now stretched across a 1,000-mile-long front, No. 60 Squadron had two Javelins at Labuan, another pair at Kuching, two more at Butterworth and four at Tengah, all on QRA. Wg Cdr Fraser was very concerned about how over-stretched the squadron was at this time stating that '.....the Javelin is not the aircraft for operating away from base without considerable technical backing'. However, the ground crew worked long hours and serviceability rates remained high thanks to their efforts.

The Indonesians became increasingly active in Borneo during April 1964 and one Javelin crew was lucky to remain unscathed when sixty 12.5 mm rounds were fired at their aircraft while they were escorting a supply drop; luckily none of them hit the fighter. A second Javelin F(AW).9, XH876, was also fired upon in the region a few weeks later and, after landing at Kuching, a single hole in an engine intake showed how close they had come to being seriously damaged. In another incident, on 16 May a pair of Javelins from Kuching played a significant role in the capture of a launch which was refusing to comply with orders from a patrol vessel to stop. However, after a couple of full reheat low passes over the launch, the captain of the launch quickly surrendered before it was boarded by crew from HMS *Wilkieston*.

Javelin F(AW).9R XH896 was hit by ground fire on 16 October during a low-level patrol over Borneo but, once again, the crew were fortunate not be injured and the damage to the aircraft was minimal. During November, the tension continued to rise and standing patrols were carried out at night over Kuala Lumpur while the Indonesians continued to enter into the Sarawak and Sabah regions. One particular incident involved the 1st Battalion, 2nd King Edward VII's Own Gurkhas, on 10 December, who were ambushed by approximately 100 guerrillas. The Gurkhas called for air support and fortunately Flt Lt R. E. Lockhart and Flt Lt S. H. Davies were already on a routine patrol out of Labuan in F(AW).9R XH908. There was no chance of using the Javelin's guns to deter the guerrillas; however, the aircraft's reheat was once again used to full effect and was lit as Lockhart flew over the Indonesians at very low level. The noise was so intense that the guerrillas thought they were being bombed and withdrew.

On 29 March 1965, Flt Lt J. S. C. Davies and Lt R. Patterson, RN in F(AW).9R XH959 flew the 1,000th operational sortie over Borneo. Incursions into Sarawak continued during April and, during one such incident, a No. 60 Squadron crew was called upon to provide air support for ground troops south of Tebedu. Unable to directly assist, the crew managed to call up a gaggle of ground attack Hunters and the problem was quickly resolved. A similar incident took place a couple of weeks later when the 2nd Battalion, Parachute Regiment, was attacked by a larger force near Pang Amo, not far from Kuching. A pair of Javelins in the air at the time made sure that a Hastings and Valetta made it safely into the region to drop supplies to the paratroopers.

No. 64 Squadron was officially reformed at Tengah on 1 April 1965, having operated as a pair of flights between Binbrook and the Singaporean airfield. Just like No. 60 Squadron, No. 64 Squadron was quickly employed to provide air defence, with one detachment covering Singapore and the Malay Peninsula and a second covering Borneo, which helped to take some pressure off No. 60 Squadron's extensive commitments. Within a few weeks, it was No. 64 Squadron's turn to perform Operation Tramp for real when a pair of scrambles was made, both of them intercepting Indonesian Tu-16s.

75 per cent of No. 64 Squadron's sorties were taken up while operating over Borneo and, in September alone, the Javelins flew 179 sorties. Advance warning of potential interceptions was always a frustration for the crews, who were given very little time to pick up aircraft crossing the Malaysian border with Kalimantan. One incident that still causes a stir to this day took place in September 1964 when a No. 64 Squadron Javelin met an Indonesian Lockheed C-130 Hercules at low level, head-on. The incident took place in a 'valley close to the border' and before the Javelin had a chance to engage, the Hercules made an evasive manoeuvre and slipped back across the border.

On Christmas Eve 1965, all of No. 64 Squadron's aircraft and groundcrew had been withdrawn from Borneo and Butterworth and were finally centralised at Tengah. This scenario was to be short-lived because problems flared up in Borneo yet again and by February 1966, No. 64 Squadron found itself back in the theatre along with No. 60 Squadron, who contributed another four Javelins, basing them at Kuching. Just a few days later, on 17 February, Flt Lt C. V. Holman and Sqn Ldr G. Moores in F(AW).9 XH777 were involved in another 'reheat' confrontation. Sqn Ldr Moores spotted some suspicious movement on the ground and so Holman began a series of low-level passes, once again using the aircraft's reheat to pin the guerrillas down. Holman kept this up for nearly 30 minutes before a nearby patrol of the 2nd Battalion, 7th Gurkha Rifles, attacked the guerrillas, resulting in one dead and five captured.

Despite the reduced tension, Tu-16 intercepts continued during the spring and early summer of 1966 before the 'confrontation' officially ended on 11 August. The very last operational Javelin sortie took place five days later and it was not long before both Nos 60 and 64 Squadrons were cut down to size. The former had been the RAF's largest Javelin squadron with thirty aircraft on strength at its peak. However, before August 1966 was over, the two squadrons had been reduced to just twelve aircraft with sixteen aircrew apiece.

Both squadrons, while still continuing Operation Tramp to a lesser degree, slumped into a period of routine, practice flying and exercises until 15 June 1967, when No. 64 Squadron was disbanded. No. 60 Squadron, who had a local reputation for large formation flying which began when celebrating their own 50th Anniversary on 30 April 1966, followed suit on 2 May 1968 with a final 'Diamond Nine'. The Javelin had worked hard in the Far East and it was most fitting that it was in this theatre that the aircraft was operationally 'bowed out'.

Cyprus 1963

Britain found itself between a rock and hard place when, in December 1963, the Greek and Turkish Cypriots began fighting. Trouble had been brewing since Cyprus had gained her independence in August 1960. No. 29 Squadron, which was based at RAF Nicosia at the time, was on the front line thanks to regular low-level passes by Turkish fighters and increasing threats on the ground from armed gangs. The squadron was relocated to the more secure RAF Akrotiri during a very short notice move, which was carried out swiftly at night, and from there began a number of operational sorties. These mainly involved flying standing patrols with the objective of stopping Turkish fighters from flying low-level incursions. No. 29 Squadron briefly returned to Nicosia, only to settle back at Akrotiri from mid-January 1964 onwards. Here, one aircraft was maintained at 2 minutes' readiness during the day and another aircraft at 10 minutes' readiness at night while a second aircraft was also kept in reserve at 30 minutes' readiness. The majority, if not all, of the Turkish aircraft were Republic F-84F Thunderstreaks and, without exception, they would drop their tanks and turn north to vacate the area once a Javelin had intercepted them. Under strict orders not to engage the Turkish Air Force aircraft once they were turning away, the No. 29 Squadron Javelins would stay with the intercept for 20 or sometimes 30 miles before being recalled back to their patrol zone or back to base. The final interception took place in April 1964; it was to be the last of sixty-two operational sorties.

Zambia/Rhodesian Crisis Dec. 1965 – Aug. 1966

Tension in southern Africa peaked when the Rhodesian Unilateral Declaration of Independence (UDI) took place on 11 November 1965. The United Kingdom's response was more political than military and began with economic sanctions, followed by the movement of military units into Zambia to make the Rhodesians think twice about attacking the Kariba Dam. No. 29 Squadron, based at RAF Akrotiri, was the nearest Javelin unit by some margin but it would still take a multi-stop, long-range operation to get the fighters to the region. Things happened fast, though, and on 19 November all flying was stopped so that long-range tanks could be fitted and, just five days later, the aircraft were already carrying out proving flights between Akrotiri and RAF Luqa. Ten Javelins were prepared for the trip while ground personnel were placed at 12-hour readiness. Led by the CO, Wg Cdr K. Burge, the ten Javelins departed Akrotiri on 28 November, travelling via Diyabakir, Dezful/Vahdati and ending the day at RAF Masirah. Onwards to RAF Khormaksar on 29 November and further south to Kenya where, at midday on 1 December, the ten Javelins arrived at Nairobi. The No. 29 Squadron detachment remained at Nairobi for three days and then nine aircraft departed for Ndola in Zambia, where they were joined by the rest of squadron, who had arrived in three No. 70 Squadron Handley Page Hastings.

Operationally, Ndola was adequate for a Javelin squadron's needs, thanks to the Zambian Air Force facilities; however, the domestic arrangements were slightly below par. The RAF would make do, but one serious commodity that was in short supply was fuel and, thanks to the United Kingdom's sanctions, Rhodesia had turned off the oil pipe into Zambia. This obviously had a direct impact on No. 29 Squadron operations and a major airlift of fuel from Aden into Zambia, via RAF Bristol Britannias, was begun. At first, there was only enough fuel for three sorties per day; as the detachment continued this situation did improve, but No. 29 Squadron operations would be continually restricted during their time in Zambia.

In order to place No. 29 Squadron much closer to Rhodesia, four aircraft were deployed to Lusaka, a mere 55 miles from the border. Compared to Ndola, Lusaka was pretty primitive; Squadron Operations was a tent while accommodation, located at the local showground, could only be described as substandard. Lusaka was located at 4,000 ft ASL and, with only

RAF Germany in the 1960s. Here we have three No. 11 Squadron Javelin F(AW).9s and a T.3 plus a batch of Canberra B(I).8s in the background. (Via E. Roffe)

a 6,600-foot-long runway, the Javelin was on the cusp of being able to actually fly out of the airfield. As a result, flying was restricted to scrambles only and a pair of aircraft were kept fully armed, one at 10 minutes', and the other at 30 minutes' readiness.

With only a couple of scrambles per month on average, against targets that never ventured near the Rhodesian border, let alone over it, morale began to decline due to the poor accommodation at Lusaka and the lack of flying. By the summer of 1966, sufficient fuel had been flown in to support up to 120 Javelin sorties per month and a combination of more rotations between Lusaka and Ndola and the increased opportunity to return to Akrotiri when an aircraft needed servicing, morale began to rise again. The Javelin had performed well in very difficult conditions and, during the nine-month-long detachment only two incidents, both as a result of undercarriage fractures, had occurred, although both aircraft were damaged beyond repair (DBR).

Fg Off. M. B. Langham and Fg Off. R. J. P. MacRae carried out the last operational scramble in Zambia on 11 August 1966 in F(AW).9R XH891. By the end of the month, No. 29 Squadron was back home at Akrotiri.

No. 33 Squadron Javelin F(AW).9 XH780 'A', pictured around the time that the squadron deployed to RAF Gütersloh in 1962. (Via E. Roffe)

No. 41 Squadron deployed their Javelin F(AW).8s to RAF Gütersloh in April 1962. (Via E. Roffe)

Above: No. 60 Squadron Javelin F(AW).9 XH722 'F' at RAF Tengah in 1966. This aircraft was SOC at RAF Seletar in July 1967. (Via E. Roffe)

Below: No. 60 Squadron Javelin F(AW).9 XH787 'G' at RAF Tengah. XH787 was written off following a heavy landing at Butterworth in May 1967. (Via E. Roffe)

Above: No. 60 Squadron Javelin FAW.9 XH707 'P' at RAF Labuan, an airfield that served as a staging post for transport aircraft of the Far East Transport Wing operating out of RAF Changi. (Via E. Roffe)

Below: No. 60 Squadron F(AW).9 XH841 'D', one of the last Javelins in operational service. (R. L. Ward Collection via C. F. Smedley)

Above: No. 60 Squadron Javelin F(AW).9 XH959 'U' at rest at Labuan. On 29 March 1965, the aircraft flew the thousandth operational sortie over Borneo. (Via E. Roffe)

Below: No. 64 Squadron operated the Javelin F(AW).9 in the Far East from 1 April 1965 until their disbandment on 15 June 1967. This is XH893 'V' touching down at Tengah. (Via E. Roffe)

Above: The arrival of No. 64 Squadron in the theatre increased the capability of the RAF in the region and reduced the pressure on the over-stretched No. 60 Squadron. This is F(AW).9 XN876 'N' of No. 64 Squadron in 1966. (Via E. Roffe)

Below: Javelin F(AW).9R XH885 'R' of No. 60 Squadron, on patrol at low level over the jungle. Transferred to No. 64 Squadron, the aircraft was lost after a start-up fire at Tengah in November 1966. (*Flight* via the R. L. Ward Collection)

Above: F(AW).9R XH877 'W' was another aircraft that served with both No. 60 Squadron (pictured) and No. 64 Squadron. The aircraft was lost when an engine exploded 20 miles north-east of Tawau, Sabah, in June 1965. (Via E. Roffe)

Below: The first production Javelin T.3, XH390 'O', during service with No. 60 Squadron. First flown on 6 January 1958, the trainer only served with the A&AEE and No. 60 Squadron during her career, which came to an end when the trainer was SOC on 1 May 1968. (Via E. Roffe)

Above: F(AW).9 XH777 'R' of No. 60 Squadron, the aircraft in which Flt Lt C. V. Holman and Sqn Ldr G. Moores spent 30 minutes carrying out low-level reheat passes in support of the 2nd Battalion, 7th Gurkha Rifles, on 17 February 1966. (Via E. Roffe)

Below: A lovely image of No. 29 Squadron Javelin F(AW).9R XH712 'K' staging through RAF Sharjah en route to Ndola in Zambia in later 1965. (Via E. Roffe)

Above: No. 29 Squadron F(AW).9R XH889 'H', one of ten Javelins captured at RAF Sharjah en route to Zambia. (Via E. Roffe)

Below: A lovely shot of No. 23 Squadron Javelin F(AW).9 XH890 'M', which was wrecked following a landing accident during the Zambian detachment. The aircraft was left behind and later used in a children's playground before it was scrapped in July 1972. (Crown Copyright via the R. L. Ward Collection)

The Second Line Units

A large number of second line RAF units and establishments operated the Javelin from 1956 through to 1975; the following describes the activities of just a few of them.

The largest operator by far (over eighty served) was No. 228 OCU, which was formed at RAF Leeming back in May 1947 to train crews in the tactical light bomber and night fighter roles. The latter tasking would extend to all-weather training to encompass the capability of the Javelin. The first Javelins to arrive were all F(AW).5s, from early 1956, which were later complemented by the T.3 trainer variant in 1958 and a few Canberra T.17s equipped with the AI Mk 17 for navigator/radar operator training. The unit, like so many large second line training establishments, had a war role and should the balloon go up, No. 228 OCU would become No. 137 Squadron. As the effects of the 1957 White Paper began to take their toll on front line fighter squadrons, No. 228 OCU's work was quickly over and, on 15 September 1961, the unit was disbanded.

One unit formed within No. 228 OCU during this first period was the JMTU (Javelin Mobile Training Unit) in February 1957. A combination of a lack of a two-seat trainer and a large number of operational squadrons waiting to convert to the Javelin resulted in this efficient mobile unit, which was under the command of ex-No. 46 Squadron pilot Sqn Ldr P. D. C. Street, DSC. The JMTU had no Javelin aircraft of its own but was made up of a pair of Javelin pilots, four navigators and a Vickers Valetta C.1 and T.4. Of the latter, one was a flying classroom with an AI Mk 17 fitting in the nose while the other served as a transport aircraft. The objective of the unit was to operate from the converting squadron's home airfield and the JMTU would run a two-week-long ground school. Ground equipment included a mocked up Javelin cockpit simulator and an AI Mk 17 caravan which housed a ground training rig for the navigator/radar operators. On top of that, the JMTU was supported by staff from Gloster Aircraft, Martin Baker and Armstrong Siddeley, who gave lectures on the airframe, ejection seats and engines respectively. Pilots of the JMTU would also be tasked with collecting new Javelins direct from Moreton Valence and/or an MU and delivering them to the squadron, where the converting pilots carried out three 'flights' in the cockpit simulator before carrying out a real familiarisation flight. Half a dozen day sorties and a single night sortie would be performed before the pilot would be declared 'operational on type'. The navigator/radar operators had to fly thirteen AI sorties before being declared operational. With the arrival of the T.3 at Leeming, the JMTU was disbanded in 1959.

Thanks to events in the Far East, No. 228 OCU got a second bite at the cherry when it was reformed at RAF Leuchars on 1 May 1965 under the command of Sqn Ldr G. Beaton AFC. Specifically tasked to train Javelin crews for overseas commands operating all-weather and night fighter squadrons, the unit was equipped with four Javelin T.3s, nine FAW.9s and three Canberra T.11s. Once again, No. 228 OCU had a war role and this time would be re-designated as No. 11 (Reserve) Squadron. This second wind for No. 228 OCU was also destined to be short and the unit disbanded again on 23 December 1966.

The CFE (Central Fighter Establishment) was originally formed at RAF Tangmere in 1944, but by October 1945 had been relocated to RAF West Raynham, where it remained during the early years of the Javelin. This unit was another big operator of the Javelin and, under the CFE umbrella, a number of smaller sub-units were created, many of them also flying the type. The extended family tree of units begins with the AWW (All-Weather Wing), which received three Javelin F(AW).1s on 3 January 1956. The AWW became the AWDS (All-Weather Development Squadron) in February 1956, which operated nearly forty Javelins during its existence, including examples of the F(AW).1, F(AW).2, F(AW).5 and F(AW).7 before it was absorbed into the AFDS (Air Fighting Development Squadron) in August 1959. The AWDS was also recognised as No. 176 (Reserve) Squadron and this same unit also included another CFE sub-unit, the AWFCS (All-Weather Fighter Combat School). Just to add to the confusion, the AWFLS (All-Weather Fighter Leaders' School) was the predecessor of the AWFCS, the Javelin first arriving on strength on 9 September 1957. The AWFCS existed until 1 July 1962, when it was re-designated as the Javelin OCS, by then only operating the Javelin F(AW).5, which was only destined to exist until 12 October 1962.

The final CFE sub-unit relevant to the Javelin was FCIRS (Fighter Command Instrument Rating Squadron) which began operating the Javelin in place of the Meteor from 29 December 1959. The Javelin element of FCIRS was moved to RAF Middleton St George on 3 August 1961 while the FCIRS was incorporated into No. 226 OCU on 1 June 1963. A spin-off unit of FCIRS was the JIRS (Javelin Instrument Rating Squadron) which, while operating the Javelin T.3, remained active until 31 December 1966.

A pair of No. 228 OCU flying instructors provide us with some scale, highlighting how big an aircraft the Javelin was. Delivered to the RAF in June 1957, F(AW).5 XH692 only served with No. 228 OCU at Leeming until 4 May 1962, when it was written off by a ground fire. (*Flight* via the R. L. Ward Collection)

Thanks to its air-to-air missile capability, the Javelin is also associated with a trio of guided weapons units. The first is the GWDS (Guided Weapons Development Squadron), which was formed at RAF Valley on 1 June 1957, originally equipped with ten Supermarine Swift F.7s. The Javelin F(AW).7 arrived not long after for Firestreak trials. The GWDS was re-designated as the GWTS (Guided Weapons Training Squadron, aka No. 1 GWTS) on 1 January 1959, still located at Valley and specialising in Firestreak trials. Yet another name change came on 1 June 1962 when the GWTS became the FCMPC (Fighter Command Missile Practice Camp), during which time up to four F(AW).7s were on strength. Being a practice camp, RAF Valley now hosted a number of detachments from home squadrons all gaining valuable experience live-firing a Firestreak missile.

Another user of the Javelin was the AFDS (Air Fighting Development Squadron), which operated from RAF Wittering, Coltishall and Binbrook during the Javelin years. The AFDS operated every mark of the Javelin with the exception of the T.3.

The establishment which operated the Javelin the longest was undoubtedly the A&AEE at RAF Boscombe Down, which flew every mark from 1952 through to 1975. It was at the A&AEE that the aircraft was really put through its paces and one of the test pilots who flew the type was Flt Lt (Later Sqn Ldr) Bernard J. Noble, who served with A Sqn from 1957 to 1959. He remembers the aircraft fondly:

> Although the Javelin was often criticised because of the prohibition on stalling and spinning, it met its specification and I thought that it was quite good for its job as a bomber destroyer. It was a big, heavy aircraft and was certainly no dogfighter, but the controls were effective and in keeping with its size and role. The speed and climb of the later marks equalled that of the Hunter 6, the airbrakes were in a class on their own, and it was a good aircraft to fly at night and on instruments. Overall, its performance was as good as the Sea Vixen and other night fighters of that generation, and it came down the approach as if it was on rails, so I know which I would prefer to fly when coming home in bad weather!

It was with the A&AEE that the very last airworthy Javelin was flown into retirement on 24 January 1974. That day, Javelin F(AW).9 XH897 was flown to Duxford for preservation and remains to this day in her original, eye-catching red and white striped finish.

No. 228 OCU Javelin F(AW).5 XA667 'O' lifts out of RAF Leeming during its second tour of duty with No. 228 OCU. This hard-working aircraft crammed a lot into its six-year career, including tours with Nos 11, 41 and 72 Squadrons and two tours with No. 228 OCU. (R. L. Ward Collection)

Above: Aircraft of No. 228 OCU were a common sight on the air show circuit during the late 1950s and early 1960s. This is F(AW).5 XA718 'S' of No. 229 OCU at RAF Valley on 14 September 1957. (R. L. Ward Collection)

Below: The personal aircraft of the Commanding Officer of No. 228 OCU from 1 May 1965 to 23 December 1966, Sqn Ldr G. Beaton AFC. His aircraft, F(AW).9 XH898 'GHB', had previously served with Nos 11 and 25 Squadrons. (Via E. Roffe)

Above: Second time around for No. 228 OCU, the primary mark of Javelin was the F(AW).9, including XH767 'F', which managed to squeeze a final a tour of duty in with No. 11 Squadron before being placed into storage at RAF Shawbury in early 1967. (Via E. Roffe)

Below: One of a number of F(AW).1s operated by the CFE at RAF West Raynham was XA568. (Via E. Roffe)

Above: CFE Javelin FAW.5 XA697 'X' at West Raynham in 1958. (Via E. Roffe)

Below: Javelin FAW.5 XA660 of the CFE in around 1958. (Via E. Roffe)

Above: Javelin T.3 XH438 'A' of FCIRS in around 1961. (Via E. Roffe)

Below: Javelin T.3 XH444 'D' of the FCIRS, an aircraft that had previously served with No. 11 Squadron at RAF Geilenkirchen. (Via E. Roffe)

Above: Javelin F(AW).7 XH901 'E' of the GWDS at RAF Valley. (Via E. Roffe)

Below: Appropriately armed with a pair of Firestreak air-to-air missiles, this is Javelin F(AW).7 XH900 'D' of the GWTS in around 1960. (Via E. Roffe)

Above: AFDS Javelin FAW.9 XH972 in the shed in the company of a pair of Lightnings and a Hunter at RAF Coltishall in 1960. (R. L. Ward Collection)

Below: A rare image of AFDS Javelin F(AW).1 XA556 'C' on final approach into RAF Coltishall on 22 August 1960. (R. L. Ward Collection)

Without exception, all marks of the Javelin would have passed through the A&AEE at RAF Boscombe Down, including F(AW).4 XA649, pictured in 1957. (Via E. Roffe)

Engine start-up problems plagued the Javelin throughout its career. In mid-1958, test pilot Flt Lt Bernard Noble of 'A' Squadron, A&AEE, experienced first-hand what a start explosion was like. F(AW).5 XA725 was repaired, going on to serve with Nos 3 and 11 Squadrons in West Germany. (Via Bernard Noble)

The A&AEE carried out a number of refuelling trials using Javelin F(AW).7 XH780 before the larger, detachable boom was fitted to the F(AW).9R. (Via Bernard Noble)

F(AW).2 XA778 spent its entire career, which lasted from August 1956 until 1968, with the A&AEE at Boscombe Down. (Via E. Roffe)

Still a few years from retirement, the A&AEE's F(AW).9 XH897 puts on a show at RAF Coningsby on 12 July 1972. (R. L. Ward Collection)

Technical Specifications

GA.5 Prototypes

Serials: WD804, WD808, WT827, WT830 and WT836
Engines: Two 7,500 lb Armstrong Siddeley Sapphire Sa.3 axial-flow turbojets; later two 8,000 lb Armstrong Siddeley Sapphire Sa.6 axial-flow turbojets.
Dimensions: Span, 52 ft; Length, 56 ft 3 in.; Height, 16 ft; Wing area, 927 sq/ft
Weights: Max., 29,200 lb
Fuel: 765 gal. (3,475 litres); two ventral tanks of 250 gal. each (1,136 litres)*
Performance: Less than Specification F.4/48

*WT827 only

F(AW).1

Serials: XA544–572 and XA618–XA628 (x 40) (Contract No.6/Aircraft/8336 – 14 July 1952)
Engines: Two 8,000 lb Armstrong Siddeley Sapphire Sa.6 Mk 10201 (port) and Mk 10301 (starboard) axial-flow turbojets
Dimensions: Span, 52 ft; Length, 56 ft 3 in.; Height, 16 ft; Wing area, 927 sq/ft
Weights: Take-off (clean), 31,580 lb; Max overload (two ventral tanks), 36,690 lb
Fuel: 765 gal. (3,475 litres); two ventral tanks of 250 gal. each (1,136 litres)
Performance: Max speed, 709 mph at sea level (clean); Max speed at 40,000 ft, 621 mph; Climb to 45,000 ft, 9.8 min.; Service ceiling, 52,500 ft; Absolute ceiling, 55,000 ft
Armament: Four 30 mm Aden guns

F(AW).2

Serials: XA768–XA814 (x 30) and XD158 F(AW).2 prototype (Contract No.6/Aircraft/8336 – 14 July 1952)
Engines: Two 8,000 lb Armstrong Siddeley Sapphire Sa.6 Mk 10701 (port) and Mk 10801 (starboard) axial-flow turbojets
Dimensions: Span, 52 ft; Length, 56 ft 3 in.; Height, 16 ft; Wing area, 927 sq/ft
Weights: Take-off (clean), 32,100 lb; Max overload (two ventral tanks), 37,200 lb
Fuel: 765 gal. (3,475 litres); two ventral tanks of 250 gal. each (1,136 litres)
Performance: Max speed, 709 mph at sea level (clean); Max speed at 40,000 ft, 621 mph; Climb to 45,000 ft, 9.8 min.; Service ceiling, 52,500 ft; Absolute ceiling, 55,000 ft
Armament: Four 30 mm Aden guns

T.3

Serials: WT841 (T.3 prototype), XH390–XH397, XH432–XH438, XH443–XH447, XK577 and XM336 (x 22) (Contract No.6/Aircraft/11262 – 27 September 1954)
Engines: Two 8,000 lb Armstrong Siddeley Sapphire Sa.6 Mk 11201 (port) and Mk 11301 (starboard) axial-flow turbojets
Dimensions: Span, 52 ft; Length, 59 ft 11 in.; Height, 16 ft; Wing area, 927 sq/ft
Weights: Take-off (clean), 38,100 lb; Max overload (two ventral tanks), 42,000 lb
Fuel: 1,064 gal. (4,836 litres); two ventral tanks of 250 gal. each (1,136 litres)
Performance: Max speed, 639 mph at sea level (clean); Max speed at 35,000 ft, 602 mph; Climb to 45,000 ft, 22 min.; Service ceiling, 46,000 ft; Absolute ceiling, 49,500 ft
Armament: Four 30 mm Aden guns

F(AW).4

Serials: XA629–XA767 (x 50) (Contract No.6/Aircraft/8336 – 14 July 1952)
Engines: Two 8,000 lb Armstrong Siddeley Sapphire Sa.6 Mk 10201 (port) and Mk 10301 (starboard) axial-flow turbojets
Dimensions: Span, 52 ft; Length, 56 ft 3 in.; Height 16 ft; Wing area, 927 sq/ft
Weights: Take-off (clean), 32,800 lb; Max overload (two ventral tanks), 37,480 lb
Fuel: 765 gal. (3,475 litres); two ventral tanks of 250 gal. each (1,136 litres)
Performance: Max speed, 702 mph at sea level (clean); Max speed at 40,000 ft, 633 mph; Climb to 45,000 ft, 8 min.; Service ceiling, 50,700 ft; Absolute ceiling, 52,000 ft
Armament: Four 30 mm Aden guns

F(AW).5

Serials: XA641–XA719 and XH687–XH692 (x 64) (Contract No.6/Aircraft/8336 – 14 July 1952 and No.6/Aircraft/11329 – 19 October 1954)
Engines: Two 8,000 lb Armstrong Siddeley Sapphire Sa.6 Mk 10201 (port) and Mk 10301 (starboard) axial-flow turbojets
Dimensions: Span, 52 ft; Length, 56 ft 3 in.; Height 16 ft; Wing area, 927 sq/ft
Weights: Take-off (clean), 34,990 lb; Max overload (two ventral tanks), 39,370 lb
Fuel: 995 gal. (4,340 litres)
Performance: Max speed, 704 mph at sea level (clean); Max speed at 40,000 ft, 616 mph; Climb to 45,000 ft, 10.3 min; Service ceiling, 50,100 ft; Absolute ceiling, 51,600 ft
Armament: Four 30 mm Aden guns

F(AW).6

Serials: XA815–XA836 and XH693–XH703 (x 33)
Engines: Two 8,000 lb Armstrong Siddeley Sapphire Sa.6 Mk 10201 (port) and Mk 10301 (starboard) axial-flow turbojets
Dimensions: Span, 52 ft; Length, 56 ft 3 in.; Height, 16 ft; Wing area, 927 sq/ft
Weights: Take-off (clean), 34,990 lb; Max overload (two ventral tanks), 39,370 lb
Fuel: 995 gal. (4,340 litres)

Performance: Max speed, 704 mph at sea level (clean); Max speed at 40,000 ft, 616 mph; Climb to 45,000 ft, 10.3 min; Service ceiling, 50,100 ft; Absolute ceiling, 51,600 ft
Armament: Four 30 mm Aden guns

F(AW).7

Serials: XH704–XH965 (x 142) (Contract No.6/Aircraft/11329 C.B.7(b) – 19 October 1954)
Engines: Two 11,000 lb Armstrong Siddeley Sapphire Sa.7 Mk 20301 (port) and Mk 20401 (starboard) axial-flow turbojets
Dimensions: Span, 52 ft; Length, 56 ft 3 in.; Height, 16 ft; Wing area, 927 sq/ft
Weights: Take-off (clean), 35,960 lb; Max overload (two ventral tanks), 40,270 lb
Fuel: 915 gal. (4,158 litres) plus provision for four 100-gal. (454 litres) tanks on pylons
Performance: Max speed, 709 mph at sea level (clean); Max speed at 40,000 ft, 621 mph; Climb to 45,000 ft, 6.6 min.; Service ceiling, 52,800 ft; Absolute ceiling, 54,100 ft
Armament: Four 30 mm Aden guns and four de Havilland Firestreak AAMs on pylons

F(AW).8

Serials: XH966–XJ165 (x 47) (Contract No.6/Aircraft/11329 – 19 October 1954)
Engines: Two 11,000 lb Armstrong Siddeley Sapphire Sa.7R Mk 20501R (port) and Mk 20601R (starboard) axial-flow turbojets (12,300 lb with reheat above 20,000 ft)
Dimensions: Span, 52 ft; Length, 56 ft 3 in.; Height, 16 ft; Wing area, 927 sq/ft
Weights: Take-off (clean), 37,410 lb; Max overload (two ventral tanks), 42,510 lb
Fuel: 950 gal. (4,318 litres) plus provision for four 100-gal (454 litres) tanks on pylons
Performance: Max speed, 702 mph at sea level (clean); Max speed at 35,000 ft, 615 mph; Climb to 50,000 ft, 9.25 min.; Service ceiling, 52,000 ft; Absolute ceiling, 54,000 ft
Armament: Four 30 mm Aden guns and four de Havilland Firestreak AAMs

F(AW).9 & 9R

Serials: Seventy-six FAW.7s were converted to FAW.9 & FAW.9R standard. These were XH707–709, XH711–713, XH715–717, XH719, XH721–725, XH747, XH749, XH751–753, XH755–774, XH776–780, XH785, XH787–788, XH791–794, XH833–836, XH839–899 and XH903–964.
Engines: Two 11,000 lb Armstrong Siddeley Sapphire Sa.7R Mk 20901R (port) and Mk 21001R (starboard) axial-flow turbojets (12,300 lb with reheat above 20,000 ft)
Dimensions: Span, 52 ft; Length, 56 ft 9 in.; Height, 16 ft; Wing area, 927 sq/ft
Weights: Take-off (clean), 38,100 lb; Max overload (two ventral tanks), 43,165 lb
Fuel: 950 gal. (4,318 litres) plus provision for four 100-gal (454 litres) tanks on pylons
Performance: Max speed, 702 mph at sea level (clean), 615 mph at 35,000 ft; Climb to 50,000 ft, 9.25 min; Service ceiling, 52,000 ft; Absolute ceiling, 54,000 ft; Range, 930 miles
Armament: Four 30 mm Aden guns and four de Havilland Firestreak AAMs

Units

Operational Units

No. 3 Sqn	*Tertius primus erit*, 'The third shall be first'
A/c	FAW.4, Jan. 1959 to Jan. 1961
Dates	RF (No. 59 Sqn renumbered) 21 Jan. 1959; DB 4 Jan. 1961
Stations	Geilenkirchen, 21 Jan. 1959
COs	Wg Cdr D. W. B. Farrar DFC, AFC; Wg Cdr A. F. Peers DFC

No. 5 Sqn	*Frangas non flectas*, 'Thou mayst break, but shall not bend me'
A/c	FAW.5, Jan. 1960 to Nov. 1962
	FAW.9, Nov. 1962 to Oct. 1965
Dates	RF (No. 68 Sqn renumbered) 21 Jan. 1959 with Meteor NF.11; re-equipped with Lightning F.6, Dec. 1965
Stations	Laarbrüch, 21 Jan. 1959; to Geilenkirchen, 11 Dec. 1962; to Binbrook, 7 Oct. 1965
COs	Wg Cdr Maxwell Scannell DFC, AFC (Feb '59); Wg Cdr F. W. Sledmere AFC (May '60); Wg Cdr M. J. E. Swiney (Jul. '62); Wg Cdr C. R. Gordon MVO (Nov. '62)

No. 11 Sqn	*Ociores acrioresque aquilis*, 'Swifter and keener than eagles'
A/c	FAW.4, Oct. 1959 to Feb. 1962
	FAW.5, Aug. 1961 to Dec. 1962
	FAW.9, Dec. 1962 to Jan. 1966
Dates	RF (No. 256 Sqn renumbered) at Geilenkirchen, 21 Jan. 1959 with Meteor NF.11; DB 11 Jan. 1966
Stations	Geilenkirchen, 21 Jan. 1959
COs	Wg Cdr J. G. Crowshaw (Oct. '59); Wg Cdr D. MacIver (Dec. '61); Wg Cdr W. J. Marriot (Jun. '64)

No. 23 Sqn	*Semper Aggressus*, 'Always on the attack'
A/c	FAW.4, Mar. 1957 to Jul. 1959
	FAW.7, Apr. 1959 to Jul. 1960 and Apr. 1962 to Sep. 1962
	FAW.9R, Apr. 1960 to Oct. 1964
Dates	Javelin replaced Venom NF.3 at Coltishall in Mar. 1957; re-equipped with Lightning F.3 at Leuchars in Aug. 1964
Stations	Horsham St Faith, 12 Oct. 1956; to Coltishall, 28 May 1957; to Horsham St Faith, 7 Sep. 1958; to Coltishall, 5 Jun. 1959; to Horsham St Faith, 31 Mar. 1960; to Coltishall, 11 Jul. 1960; to Leuchars, 9 Mar. 1963

COs	Wg Cdr A. N. Davis DSO, DFC (Jul. '55); Wg Cdr J. E. Kilduff (Aug. '57); Wg Cdr G. I. Chapman AFC; Wg Cdr D. B. Wills DFC (Jun. '61); Wg Cdr A. J. Owen DFC, AFC, DFM (May '62)
No. 25 Sqn	*Feriens tego*, 'Striking I defend'
A/c	FAW.7, Dec. 1958 to Jan. 1961
	FAW.9, Dec. 1959 to Dec. 1962
Dates	Javelin replaced Meteor NF.12 and NF.14 at Waterbeach from Dec. 1958; DB at Leuchars, 31 Dec. 1962
Stations	Waterbeach, 2 Jul. 1958; to Leuchars, 30 Oct. 1961
COs	Sqn Ldr J. C. Cox (–Jan. '60); Wg Cdr J. H. Walton, AFC (Jan. '60); Wg Cdr P. G. K. Williamson, DFC (–Nov. '62)
No. 29 Sqn	*Impiger et Acer*, 'Energetic and keen'
A/c	FAW.6, Nov. 1957 to Aug. 1961
	FAW.9, Apr. 1961 to May 1967
Dates	Javelin replaced the Meteor NF.11 at Acklington from Nov. 1957; Meteor NF.12 continued to be operated between Feb. and 1958 at Leuchars; re-equipped with Lightning F.3 at Wattisham in May 1967
Stations	Acklington, 14 Jan. 1957; to Leuchars, 22 Jul. 1958; to Nicosia, 1 Mar. 1963; to Akrotiri, 16 Mar. 1964; to Ndola, 3 Dec. 1965; det. Lusaka; to Akrotiri, 3 Sep. 1966; to Wattisham, 10 May 1967
COs	Wg Cdr J. A. C. Aiken (Jan. '56); Wg Cdr W. Harbison, AFC (Jan. '58); Wg Cdr A. R. Gordon-Cumming (Jul. '59); Wg Cdr R. E. Gardiner, DFC (Jul. '61); Wg Cdr E. G. P. Jeffrey (Apr. '62); Wg Cdr K. Burge (Jan. '65); Wg Cdr R. Neil (Nov. '66); Sqn Ldr L. A. Boyer (May '67); Wg Cdr L. W. Phipps, AFC (Sep. '67)
No. 33 Sqn	Loyalty
A/c	FAW.7, Jul. 1958 to Jan. 1962
	FAW.9, Oct. 1960 to Nov. 1962
Dates	Javelin replaced Meteor NF.14 at Leeming from Jul. 1958; DB 31 Dec. 1962
Stations	Leeming, 30 Sep. 1957; to Middleton St George, 30 Sep. 1958
COs	Wg Cdr N. Poole (–Apr. '60); Wg Cdr D. L. Hughes, DFC, AFC (Apr. '60)
No. 41 Sqn	Seek and Destroy
A/c	FAW.4, Feb. 1958 to Feb. 1960
	FAW.5, Aug. 1958 to Feb. 1960
	FAW.8, Nov. 1959 to Dec. 1963
Dates	RF at Coltishall (No. 141 Sqn renumbered), Feb. 1 1958; DB 31 Dec. 1963
Stations	Coltishall, Feb. 1958; to Wattisham, 5 Jul 1958
COs	Wg Cdr W. J. Leggett (Jan. '58); Wg Cdr D. W. H. Smith (Oct. '59); Wg Cdr J. F. Pinnington (Dec. '61)
No. 46 Sqn	We rise to conquer
A/c	FAW.1, Feb. 1956 to Aug. 1957
	FAW.2, Aug. 1957 to Jun. 1961
	FAW.6, May 1958 to Oct. 1958

Dates	Javelin replaced Meteor NF.12 and NF.14 at Odiham; DB 30 Jun. 1961, nucleus remained to ferry aircraft to the Far East for No. 60 Sqn
Stations	Odiham, 15 Aug. 1954; Waterbeach, 17 Jul. 1959
COs	Wg Cdr F. E. W. Birchfield (Mar. '55); Wg Cdr H. E. White (Jun. '56); Wg Cdr F. B. Sowrey (May '58); Wg Cdr D. B. Wills (Jun. '60)

No. 60 Sqn	*Per ardua ad aethera tendo*, 'I strive through difficulties to the sky'
A/c	FAW.9, Jul. 1961 to Apr. 1968
Dates	Javelin replaced Meteor NF.14 from Jul. 1961 at Tengah; DB 2 May 1968
Stations	Tengah, 31 May 1950; dets Butterworth, Kuching, Labuan and Kai Tak
COs	Wg Cdr P. Smith, MBE (Apr. '61); Wg Cdr J. Fraser, AFC (May '65); Wg Cdr M. H. Miller, AFC (Nov. '65)

No. 64 Sqn	*Tenax propositi*, 'Firm of purpose'
A/c	FAW.7, Aug. 1958 to Oct. 1960
	FAW.9, Jul. 1960 to Jun. 1967
Dates	Javelin replaced Meteor NF.12 and NF.14 at Duxford from Aug. 1958; DB 15 Jun. 1967
Stations	Duxford, 15 Aug. 1951; to Waterbeach, 17 Jul. 1961; to Binbrook, 24 Aug. 1962; to Tengah, 1 Apr. 1965; dets Kuching and Labuan
COs	Sqn Ldr C. G. Maughan (Apr. '59)

No. 72 Sqn	Swift
A/c	FAW.4, Apr. 1959 to Jun. 1961
	FAW.5, Jun. 1959 to Jun. 1961
Dates	Javelin replaced Meteor NF.12 and NF.14 at Church Fenton from Apr. 1959; DB 30 Jun. 1961
Stations	Church Fenton, 9 May 1953; to Leconfield, 28 Jun. 1959
COs	Wg Cdr V. G. Owen-Jones, DFC (Apr. '59); Wg Cdr R. E. Gardiner, DFC (Jun. '60)

No. 85 Sqn	*Nocto Diuque Venamur*, 'We hunt by day and night'
A/c	FAW.2, Nov. 1958 to Mar. 1960
	FAW.6, Nov. 1958 to Jun. 1960
	FAW.8, Mar. 1960 to Mar. 1963
Dates	RF at Stradishall (No. 89 Sqn renumbered) 30 Nov. 1958; DB 31 Mar. 1963
Stations	Stradishall, 30 Nov. 1958; to West Malling, 5 Jun. 1959; to West Raynham, 6 Sep. 1960
COs	Wg Cdr L. G. Martin (–Oct. '58); Wg Cdr G. A. Martin (–Mar. '60); Wg Cdr S. J. Perkins, AFC (Mar. '60); Wg Cdr D. A. P. Saunders-Davies (Dec. '61)

No. 87 Sqn	*Maximus me metuit*, 'The most powerful fear me'
A/c	FAW.1, Aug. 1957 to Jan. 1961
	FAW.4, Nov. 1959 to Jan. 1961
	FAW.5, Sep. 1958 to Oct. 1960
Dates	Javelin replaced Meteor NF.11 at Brüggen from Aug. 1957 (a/c from No. 46 Sqn); DB 3 Jan. 1961

| Stations | Brüggen, Jul. 2 1957 |
| COs | Wg Cdr L. W. G. Gill, DSO (Mar. '56); Wg Cdr G. C. Lamb (1957) |

No. 89 Sqn	*Dei Auxilio Telis Meis*, 'By the help of God with my own weapons'
A/c	FAW.2, Oct. 1957 to Nov. 1958
	FAW.6, Sep. 1957 to Nov. 1958
Dates	Javelin replaced Venom NF.3 at Stradishall from Sep. 1957; DB (renumbered as No. 85 Sqn) 30 Nov. 1958
Stations	Stradishall, 15 Dec. 1955
COs	Wg Cdr G. Martin, DFC, AFC (1957)

No. 96 Sqn	*Nocturni obambulamus*, 'We prowl by night'
A/c	FAW.4, Sep. 1958 to Jan. 1959
Dates	Javelin replaced Meteor NF.11 at Geilenkirchen from Sep. 1958; DB (renumbered as No. 3 Sqn) 21 Jan. 1959
Stations	Geilenkirchen, 12 Feb. 1958
COs	Wg Cdr H. B. Verity (Jan. 1959)

No. 141 Sqn	*Caedimus Noctu*, 'We slay by night'
A/c	FAW.4, Feb. 1957 to Jan. 1958
Dates	Javelin replaced Venom NF.3 at Horsham St Faith from Feb .1957; DB (renumbered No. 41 Sqn) 1 Feb. 1958
Stations	Horsham St Faith, 14 Oct. 1956; to Coltishall, 28 May 1957

No. 151 Sqn	*Foy pour devoir*, 'Fidelity unto duty'
A/c	FAW.5, Jun. 1957 to Sep. 1961
Dates	Javelin replaced Venom NF.3 at Turnhouse in Jun. 1957; DB 19 Sep. 1961
Stations	Turnhouse, 17 Jun. 1957; to Leuchars, 15 Nov. 1957
COs	Sqn Ldr Boardman (Oct 56); Sqn Ldr J. W. Frost (Mar 58); Sqn Ldr L. C. P. Martin (Oct 58); Wg Cdr D O Luke (Jan 61)

Operational Order Into Service (Feb. 1956–Dec. 1962)

Feb 56	No. 46 Sqn	FAW.1
Feb. '57	No. 141 Sqn	FAW.4
Mar. '57	No. 23 Sqn	FAW.4
Jun. '57	No. 151 Sqn	FAW.5
Aug. '57	No. 46 Sqn	FAW.2
Aug. '57	No. 87 Sqn	FAW.1
Sep. '57	No. 89 Sqn	FAW.6
Oct. '57	No. 89 Sqn	FAW.2
Oct. '57	No. 228 OCU	T.3
Nov. '57	No. 29 Sqn	FAW.6
Feb. '58	No. 41 Sqn	FAW.4
May 58	No. 46 Sqn	FAW.6
Jul. '58	No. 33 Sqn	FAW.7
Aug. '58	No. 41 Sqn	FAW.5

Aug. '58	No. 64 Sqn	FAW.7
Sep. '58	No. 87 Sqn	FAW.5
Sep. '58	No. 96 Sqn	FAW.4
Nov. '58	No. 85 Sqn	FAW.2
Nov. '58	No. 85 Sqn	FAW.6
Dec. '58	No. 25 Sqn	FAW.7
Jan. '59	No. 3 Sqn	FAW.4
Apr. '59	No. 23 Sqn	FAW.7
Apr. '59	No. 72 Sqn	FAW.4
Jun. '59	No. 72 Sqn	FAW.5
Oct. '59	No. 11 Sqn	FAW.4
Nov. '59	No. 41 Sqn	FAW.8
Nov. '59	No. 87 Sqn	FAW.4
Dec. '59	No. 25 Sqn	FAW.9
Jan. '60	No. 5 Sqn	FAW.5
Mar. '60	No. 85 Sqn	FAW.8
Apr. '60	No. 23 Sqn	FAW.9R
Jul. '60	No. 64 Sqn	FAW.9
Oct. '60	No. 33 Sqn	FAW.9
Apr. '61	No. 29 Sqn	FAW.9
Jul. '61	No. 60 Sqn	FAW.9
Aug. '61	No. 11 Sqn	FAW.5
Nov. '62	No. 5 Sqn	FAW.9
Dec. '62	No. 11 Sqn	FAW.9

Glossary

A&AEE	Aeroplane & Armament Experimental Establishment
ADIZ	Air Defence Identification Zone
AFC	Air Force Cross
AFDS	Air Fighting Development Squadron
AI	Air Interception
AW	All Weather
AWW	All Weather Wing
AWDS	All Weather Development Squadron
AWFCS	All Weather Fighter Combat School
AWFLS	All Weather Fighter Leaders School
CA	Certificate of Airworthiness
CFCS	Central Fighter Combat School
CFE	Central Fighter Establishment
CSE	Central Signals Establishment
DB	Disbanded
DBR	Damaged Beyond Repair
DFC	Distinguished Flying Cross
DSO	Distinguished Service Order
DTD	Directorate of Technical Development
ETPS	Empire Test Pilots School
FCIRF/S	Fighter Command Instrument Rating Flight/Squadron
FCMPC	Fighter Command Missile Practice Camp
FCTU	Fighter Command Trials Unit
Fg Off.	Flying Officer
Flt Lt	Flight Lieutenant
FRL	Flight Refuelling Ltd
FU	Ferry Unit
GA	Gloster Aircraft
Gp	Group
GWDS	Guided Weapons Development Squadron
GWTS	Guided Weapons Trials Squadron
JIRS	Javelin Instrument Rating Squadron
JMCU	Javelin Mobile Conversion Unit
JOCS	Javelin Operational Conversion Squadron
MoS	Ministry of Supply

MU	Maintenance Unit
NATO	North Atlantic Treaty Organisation
NF	Night Fighter
OCU	Operation Conversion Unit
OR	Operational Requirement
QRA	Quick Reaction Alert
RAE	Royal Aircraft Establishment
RF	Reformed
RN	Royal Navy
RNAS	Royal Naval Air Station
SOC	Struck off Charge
Sqn Ldr	Squadron Leader
Wg Cdr	Wing Commander

Bibliography

Halley, James J. (ed.), *RAF Aircraft WA100–WZ999* (Air Britain).

Halley, James J. (ed.), *RAF Aircraft XA100–XZ999* (Air Britain).

James, Derek N., *Gloster Aircraft Since 1917* (Putnam).

Jefford, C. G., *RAF Squadrons* (Airlife).

Mason, Francis K., *The British Fighter Since 1912* (Putnam).

Napier, Michael, *Gloster Javelin: An Operational History* (Pen & Sword).

Rawlings, John D. R., *Fighter Squadrons of the RAF* (Macdonald).

Sturtivant, Ray, with John Hamlin, *Flying Training and Support Aircraft Since 1912* (Air Britain).

Thetford, Owen, *Aircraft of the Royal Air Force Since 1918* (Putnam).

Webb, Derek Collier, *UK Flight Testing Accidents 1940–71* (Air Britain).